Brent Q. Hafen, Ph.D., a professor of Health
Science at Brigham Young University,
has written several books in the fields
of emergency care, food, nutrition, alcohol abuse,
drugs, and related health topics.

Brenda Peterson, M.S., a technical editor
at TRW Defense and Space Systems, Inc.,
has written books on first aid, rape, abortion,
human maturation, and microprocessor typography.

BRENT Q. HAFEN
and BRENDA PETERSON
with Kathryn J. Frandsen

THE CRISIS INTERVENTION HANDBOOK

A SPECTRUM BOOK

Prentice-Hall, Inc., Englewood Cliffs, New Jersey 07632

Library of Congress Cataloging in Publication Data

Hafen, Brent Q.
    The crisis intervention handbook.

    (A Spectrum Book)
    Includes index.
    1. Crisis intervention (Psychiatry)   I. Peterson,
Brenda.   II. Frandsen, Kathryn J.   III. Title.
RC480.6.H33   616.89'025   82-3637
                                        AACR2
ISBN 0-13-193755-3 (pbk)
ISBN 0-13-193763-4

10 9 8 7 6 5 4 3 2 1

Editorial/production supervision by Claudia Citarella
Manufacturing buyer: Barbara Frick

This Spectrum Book is available to businesses and organizations
at a special discount when ordered in large quantities.
For information, contact Prentice-Hall, Inc., General Publishing
Division, Special Sales, Englewood Cliffs, New Jersey 07632.

ISBN 0-13-193755-3 {PBK.}

ISBN 0-13-193763-4

Prentice-Hall International, Inc., *London*
Prentice-Hall of Australia Pty. Limited, *Sydney*
Prentice-Hall of Canada, Ltd., *Toronto*
Prentice-Hall of India Private Limited, *New Delhi*
Prentice-Hall of Japan, Inc., *Tokyo*
Prentice-Hall of Southeast Asia Pte. Ltd., *Singapore*
Whitehall Books Limited, *Wellington, New Zealand*

CONTENTS

INTRODUCTION   ix

1

PRINCIPLES OF CRISIS INTERVENTION   1

WHO EXPERIENCES CRISES? 2
ELEMENTS OF CRISIS INTERVENTION, 3
PREDICTABLE CRISES, 5
UNPREDICTABLE CRISES, 5
SUPPORT SYSTEMS, 6
EFFECTING CHANGE IN CRISIS, 9
WORKING WITH CHILDREN IN CRISIS, 13
SIGNS AND SYMPTOMS OF CRISIS, 14
HELPING YOURSELF, 16

2

DEATH AND DYING   18

EMOTIONAL STAGES OF DYING, 19
NEEDS OF THE DYING PERSON, 22
RIGHTS OF THE DYING PERSON, 24
MEETING NEEDS OF THE DYING, 25
EXPLAINING DEATH TO CHILDREN, 28
HELPING A CHILD FACE DEATH, 29

3

GRIEF AND MOURNING   35

NORMAL GRIEF REACTIONS, 36   ANTICIPATORY GRIEF, 40
ABNORMAL GRIEF, 41   WHAT YOU CAN DO TO HELP, 41
BEREAVED CHILDREN, 42   HOW TO HELP A BEREAVED CHILD, 45
GRIEVING PARENTS, 49   THE DEATH OF INFANTS, 50
SUDDEN INFANT DEATH SYNDROME, 52   LOSING A SPOUSE, 54

4

EUTHANASIA   56

ARGUMENTS FOR EUTHANASIA, 64
ARGUMENTS AGAINST EUTHANASIA, 67

5

ABORTION   70

REASONS FOR ABORTION, 70
ADJUSTMENTS TO PREGNANCY/ABORTION, 72
HOW CAN YOU HELP? 75   ABORTION AND SUICIDE, 78
REFUSING TO GRANT AN ABORTION, 78

6

CHILD ABUSE   80

FACTORS LEADING TO CHILD ABUSE, 81
IDENTIFYING CHILD ABUSE, 83   HOW YOU CAN HELP, 83

7

RAPE AND SEXUAL ASSAULT   88

HOW A WOMAN REACTS TO RAPE, 89
HELPING THE RAPE VICTIM RECOVER, 92

8

PSYCHIATRIC EMERGENCIES   97

PRINCIPLES OF MANAGEMENT, 100

9

DEPRESSION   107

SIGNS AND SYMPTOMS OF DEPRESSION, 108
DEPRESSION IN CHILDREN, 110
DEPRESSION IN ADOLESCENTS, 111
POSTNATAL DEPRESSION, 112   HOW TO HELP, 116
PREVENTION OF DEPRESSION, 117

10

SUICIDE   118

SUICIDE AMONG ADOLESCENTS, 122
SUICIDE AMONG THE ELDERLY, 129
SUICIDE PREVENTION, 131

11

EMOTIONAL ASPECTS OF ILLNESS   134

WHAT YOU CAN DO TO HELP, 135

12

DRUG AND ALCOHOL EMERGENCIES   141

FACTORS MAKING ABUSE MORE SERIOUS, 142
WHAT YOU CAN DO TO HELP, 143

HANDLING A HOSTILE PERSON, 145
MEDICAL DANGER SIGNS, 145
FIRST AID MEASURES, 146

13

DISASTERS   148

PHASES OF DISASTER, 150   WHO IS INVOLVED? 152
GENERAL GUIDELINES FOR DISASTER MANAGEMENT, 154
GROUPS WITH SPECIAL NEEDS, 156
FOUR PRINCIPLES TO REMEMBER, 160

INDEX   163

INTRODUCTION

Anyone can experience a crisis—the man next door, the woman at the office, the child who lives in the house on the corner, your sister. Even you can experience a crisis. A *crisis* occurs when emotional pressure becomes so great than an individual's own ability to handle the pressure is reduced or lost.

A certain succession of crisis events is a normal part of every person's life, and the crisis brought about by change and loss is important to normal social and emotional growth. Each of us can expect to experience the loss of people who are important to us (either through a change in the nature of the relationship or through death), the loss of objects, and perhaps the loss of social status or physical health. These losses are a natural part of change; to encompass the promise of gain, change must also involve the certainty of painful loss. And change is an inherent part of growth—growth is a dynamic process that can't occur without change.

This book is about things we can each do to make the way smoother, things we can each do to help ourselves and others cope and adjust to change and the loss that accompanies it during difficult periods of our lives. It contains information on how to deal with normal crises that affect every human being, such as death, as well as information on how to deal with less common emotional stress resulting from experiences such as rape, child abuse, suicide, and alcohol abuse.

The principles in this book encompass a form of first aid: psychological first aid, the ability to provide emotional support to an individual during a vulnerable crisis period in his life that will enable him to make a healthy adjustment and continue in his growth. Psychological first aid principles will enable you to reduce or prevent physical and emotional harm to people in crisis and to those who are near them. Psychological first aid is a lot like medical first aid; its goals are to halt the immediate traumatic process, to prevent further injury or stress, and to save lives.

Any person can readily learn the principles of psychological first aid; it is a short-term, immediate type of help that does not involve psychotherapy or psychiatric counseling. Through mastery of the principles of psychological first aid you will be able to help others manage stress situations, and you will be able to exercise rational self-counseling during periods of stress in your own life.

The fundamental techniques in this book will give you a firm foundation toward developing the skills to effectively deal with yourself and others in the face of change, loss, and the crisis that sometimes accompanies both.

PRINCIPLES OF CRISIS INTERVENTION

Life naturally involves the need to solve problems. Every new situation we encounter requires us to devise novel ways of tapping our inner strength and of working with our environment to resolve conflict. Often it takes a number of unsuccessful attempts before we discover the best and most workable solutions to our problems. By learning to develop and use new and different resources we discover problem-solving methods that we can use again when similar problems arise.

But sometimes, as a normal part of every person's life, problems and changes are temporarily beyond a person's capacity to cope. When the problem is extremely difficult, or when the individual's support system either within himself or from others is inadequate, he is thrown off balance emotionally; we refer to this as a *crisis*.

Crisis, then, can be the result of one or more factors: a problem arises that is too great or overwhelming; a problem carries special significance that makes it overwhelming; a problem occurs at a time of special vulnerability; a problem occurs when the individual's normal coping mechanisms are blocked for any reason; a problem occurs for which a person is unprepared; or a problem occurs at a time when others are unable to help and support the person.

Crisis is always time limited; it may last for only a few hours, or it may stretch into a period of a few months. Most crises occur within ten days to two weeks of the event that causes the stress;[1] the most lengthy period of crisis, that associated with the death of a loved one, normally runs its course in about six weeks;[2] and a person who is unable to begin healing after that time may require more extensive professional help.[3]

Crisis is not always bad; it represents a pivotal point in an individual's life, and it brings opportunity as well as danger. In a person's search for an adequate method of coping he may choose a course of destruction or may choose to explore and develop new and more effective methods than he had previously known. Crisis itself brings to each of us the potential for positive growth and change.

Crisis intervention is a term used to describe the kind of psychological first aid that enables you to help an individual, group, or family experiencing a temporary loss of ability to cope with a problem or situation.[4] It can include help rendered in an unusual emergency, such as rape, or assistance with everyday problems that affect everyone.

WHO EXPERIENCES CRISES?

All stable persons of any age are susceptible to emotional trauma; some are more crisis-prone than others, but this does not mean that they are mentally or physically ill. Any person's vulnerability to emotional trauma depends on how new, intense, and long-lasting the stresses are.[5] Of course, crises occur more commonly among those who are genuinely emotionally ill, but those individuals require long-term professional help beyond the scope of immediate psychological first aid.

Six major sources of support for every person help him cope with difficulties in life:[6]

---

[1] *Crisis Intervention,* distributed by Department of Human Development and Services, UCLA Extension.

[2] John B. Shultz, *Emergency Department Drug Abuse Treatment Technician's Booklet,* National Institute on Drug Abuse.

[3] *Crisis Intervention.*

[4] Shultz, *Emergency Department Drug Abuse Treatment Technician's Booklet.*

[5] Daniel Johnston, "Crisis Intervention Skills," *Journal of Practical Nursing,* January 1978, 16-19.

[6] *Comprehensive Emergency Services Training Guide,* Second Edition, National Center for Comprehensive Emergency Services to Children (Washington, D.C.: U.S. Department of Health, Education, and Welfare, 1977), DHEW Publication No. (OHDS) 77-30121, p. 18.

1. *Intellectual functions.*   A person's ability to act decisively, to use problem-solving techniques, and to anticipate certain stressful events greatly enhances his ability to cope with those stressful events when they do occur. Many people are able not only to anticipate stress but to prepare for it.

2. *Interpersonal assets.*   Those who are best able to cope with change and loss are generally people who can rely on others for help; they possess friends and family members who offer support in times of trial.

3. *Emotional resources.*   While it is important to be able to rely on others for help it is equally important to be able to face your own problems, not always to expect others to "bail you out." The ability to cope well is directly associated with the ability to endure uncertainty; it's important, too, to allow yourself to express your emotions freely.

4. *Hope.*   Having a reason for living and for overcoming problems is essential to the coping process.

5. *Self-motivation.*   Others can do a great deal to support you, but you must have a desire to take care of yourself and to overcome difficult problems. You must want to come out the winner! You must be able to make and carry out practical plans for solving problems, even though you may occasionally need help in forming or implementing your plans.

6. *Healthy personality.*   Your basic personality contributes to your ability to overcome crises. Those who are able to ask for help, who are willing to use help, who can make decisions, who enjoy challenge, and who readily learn from past experience are best able to cope under stress and difficulty.

ELEMENTS OF CRISIS SITUATION

Four distinct phases combine to create a crisis state:[7]

1. A problem or stress occurs in a person's life; as a natural result of the problem or stress the individual feels anxious and may become disorganized in dealing with the problem. The person will begin to try methods of dealing with the situation that have worked in the past.

2. The old methods of coping don't work—and the problem or stress continues. The individual's anxiety gets worse.

3. The individual tries other solutions as his tension deepens. Sometimes the crisis itself lessens at this point—the crisis may change in nature, or the individual may change his goals or hopes for the outcome.

[7] *Crisis Intervention.*

4. In the final phase the person, in effect, "gives up." He has tried solving his problem with all the methods he can devise himself, and nothing has worked. Anxiety and tension often lead to depression in this last stage.

The crisis itself has four distinct elements:[8]

1. *The hazardous event.* Linda, who is still adjusting to the rigors of a new marriage, gives birth and is suddenly faced with the demands and changes the baby brings. Kevin, who has been active in sports all his life, shatters his ankle in an automobile accident, ending a promising career in professional football. Ellen, widowed in her early thirties and responsible for the support of her four children, is laid off as a result of financial hardships suffered by her employer. Dean loses his wife to cancer. Paul and Cheryl, faced with temporary unemployment, are unable to qualify for financial assistance from the government.

All of these people have one thing in common: the hazardous event, the initial occurrence that starts the chain of reactions that lead to a crisis. For some it is a sudden, unexpected event such as serious illness, accident, death, or sudden loss of employment.[9] For others, the event is part of a normal developmental change: the assumption of a new role, the learning of a new task, the adjustment to new conditions.

2. *The vulnerable state.* Not all hazardous events turn into crises; the individual must be vulnerable for a crisis to develop. Illness, anxiety, or depression can make a person less able to cope with problems than usual.

3. *The precipitating factor.* The precipitating factor is, figuratively, the straw that breaks the camel's back—the final blow that makes a vulnerable person break. When Betty's two-year-old daughter was hit and killed by a speeding car in front of the house she seemed to hold up admirably; she sailed through the funeral and the days following like a pillar of strength. One day her husband arrived home to find her in a heap, sobbing at the foot of the bed. The problem? The washing machine had overflowed, flooding the laundry room. The washing machine, of course, was only the last straw—the real problem was the death of the baby.

4. *The state of active crisis.* When a person is no longer able to handle the situation a state of active crisis develops. There are some signs common to this state. A person may attempt to escape through drugs, alcohol, or excessive sleep. He generally cannot solve problems or make decisions, even those unrelated to the hazard at hand. He may appear to be in a daze or may behave in bizarre ways. Inside, he is feeling helpless, impotent, powerless, indecisive, and panicked.

It's sometimes easiest to help a person who has entered an active state of

---

[8] *Comprehensive Emergency Services Training Guide,* p. 19.

[9] *Crisis Intervention.*

crisis—who has bottomed out, so to speak. Commonly, those who are most anxious and suffering the greatest crises are most motivated to make meaningful changes in their lives.

PREDICTABLE CRISES

Events that are part of the planned, expected, or normal processes of life can lead to crises, even though they are predictable. You can see them coming and can plan and prepare for them; you can even rehearse in your mind what you will do to cope with them. John, realizing that his retirement was only ten years away, developed over those years an interest in English literature, a hobby of woodworking, and skill at freshwater fishing. Faced with the loss of his employment he felt secure with his options; he had interests and hobbies that could make his life meaningful regardless of his health. If he stayed healthy and active he could enjoy fishing and woodworking; if he became ill he could read and study.

Some predictable crises are related to development. Children must learn certain tasks; adolescents must bridge the gap into adulthood. College graduates must adjust to a first job. Law school hopefuls must take an entrance examination. These predictable crises allow us time to plan—and flexible, realistic plans reduce stress and anxiety.

Marriage, pregnancy, and retirement seem to be the most stressful times in adult life and often lead to predictable crises.

UNPREDICTABLE CRISES

An earthquake that levels a town, amputation of a leg in an industrial accident, sudden death of a parent, unexpected loss of a job—all are examples of unpredictable crises, events that are not expected and that present extraordinary challenge. There are seven major categories of unpredictable crises.[10]

1. *Crime.* Extreme stress reactions are often suffered by victims of crime, especially when the crime was against the person, such as rape, murder, or armed robbery. Added stress occurs at the police station; at the height of stress and anxiety the victim is often forced to relive the incident by giving details of the crime to investigating officers. As police officers attempt to locate and arrest the criminal the victim is often reminded of the incident by repeated questioning.

2. *Natural disaster.* The suddenness and impact of natural disasters such as

---

[10]Morton Bard, *Family Crisis Intervention: From Concept to Implementation*, U.S. Department of Justice, December 1973.

fires, floods, explosions, earthquakes, and tornadoes can lead to a crisis state among large groups of people, a situation called the disaster syndrome. Specific techniques are used with people who have been victims of a natural disaster.

3. *Notification.* When a family member has been injured or killed in an accident or when a relative dies as the result of an illness, someone must notify the other family members or the next of kin. With proper training and consideration the person who notifies can help family members deal with the crisis, even though the notification itself leads to the crisis.

4. *Accident.* Injury or death in an automobile, by a falling power line, or while swimming results in a much different kind of crisis than injury or death in an earthquake or flood. In a natural disaster the entire environment is upset, and those involved are subjected to widespread chaos. In an accident, however, the chaos is very personal and occurs in an environment that is otherwise stable and ordered.

5. *Psychotic reactions.* Genuine mental or emotional illness usually profoundly affects family members. A woman will experience a crisis, for instance, when her formerly healthy husband becomes paranoid, sleeping with a gun under his pillow and forbidding her to open the curtains during the daytime.

6. *Suicides and attempted suicides.* Suicide, like psychotic reactions, has a profound impact on those who are left behind. Attempted suicide indicates a severe crisis state.

7. *Unexpected or tragic family life experiences.* Death, divorce, and separation seem to cause the greatest crises among family members. Other situations common to many families can cause crises: departure of a family member on an extended trip, achievement of an honor or award, marriage of a family member, or social rejection of a family member.[11]

SUPPORT SYSTEMS

Our ability to cope with a difficult or stressful situation depends to a great extent on the support systems, both internal and external, that are available to us. The strengths and weaknesses within ourselves and within those around us determine what course of action we take when confronted with overwhelming situations.[12] A well-developed support system consists of five basic compo-

---

[11] Gabriel Smilkstein, "The Family in Trouble—How to Tell," *Journal of Family Practice*, 2, no. 1 (1975), 19-24.

[12] Donna C. Aquilera and Janice M. Messick, *Crisis Intervention Theory and Methodology* (St. Louis: C.V. Mosby Co., 1974), 2nd Edition.

nents: self-esteem, perception of events, social network, coping mechanisms, and economic resources.

Self-Esteem

The way you feel about yourself usually doesn't make much difference in regular, everyday situations that involve no stress; but when stress enters the picture people who don't feel good about themselves usually buckle under much more quickly and with much less stress. People who have negative self-images and who feel unable to deal with their environment are usually not as capable of expressing their needs or defending themselves.

In contrast, people with high self-esteem actually perform better under stress.[13] An effective way to bolster self-esteem is to think about a plan for predictable crises; for example, you will have confidence when your baby is born if you have planned ahead for changes in your schedule, changes in your relationship with your spouse, and reactions of your three-year-old. You will have realistic expectations of your performance, and you can move ahead with confidence in yourself.[14]

Perception of Events

Events themselves are not good or bad—the way we perceive events makes the difference. Walt had worked hard at his advertising firm and had spent four years restoring a hundred-year-old house when he received the opportunity to transfer to Chicago for a prestigious position with a national company; he looked forward to the opportunity, excited about the chance for travel and the prospect of restoring another old home. For Walt the move was not a crisis. Bill, who had been fired from his job in the Northwest because of poor performance, finally landed another job in Texas after months of demoralizing interviews and rejections. He approached the new job and the change in environment with tension and anxiety, unsure of his ability to perform satisfactorily. For Bill the move was a crisis.

Our own perception can cause other kinds of crises as well. An "anniversary crisis" is one that occurs a year after an unsettling event; a man who remained in control through his seemingly difficult divorce may crumble the next year. Crises may also occur because an unrelated event reminds us of a past conflict. Martha, remembering that her best friend was killed in an accident in Atlanta years earlier, may develop a crisis when visiting Atlanta on an exciting business trip.

[13] Brent Q. Hafen, Alton L. Thygerson, and Ronald L. Rhodes, *Prescriptions for Health* (Provo: Brigham Young University Press, 1977), p. 33.

[14] Hafen, et al., *Prescriptions for Health*, p. 36.

Our own jaded perception can also cause us wrongly to anticipate an event and actually to plan for something that will never happen. Carol, convinced that her husband was about to leave her, went through all the stages of grief—she was depressed, she became preoccupied with her husband, she reviewed in her mind all the ways he might leave her, and she adjusted by anticipating everything she would do after he left. Carol's crisis occurred when her husband stayed; she had adjusted to his leaving when he had never planned to leave.[15]

Social Network

The way each of us reacts to stress depends on a number of influences; among the most powerful are the social influences brought about by our family members, our social class, our ethnic group, and the culture around us.[16]

As humans we depend deeply on those around us to bolster us and give us help in times of trouble. We *need* friends and family members to rally around us during difficult times, sharing in our grief, our pain, or the expense of our situation—in other words, we need others to support us. The grief and pain associated with the death of a family member is not so difficult to bear when you know all other members of the family share in your sorrow.

When this social network breaks down—when there are no friends or family members to be supportive—the individual is left feeling vulnerable, alone, weak, threatened.

One of the most important of all support systems is the family. When Jill became pregnant as a teenager her family, ashamed and angry, forced her to leave home, rent a tiny, poorly furnished apartment, and support herself and her child. The lack of support in Jill's family created for her a crisis. In contrast, Kim's family worked together to prepare for the birth of her baby, sacrificing a small bedroom to be converted as a nursery and making it a family project to paint and decorate the room. The support Kim received from her family gave her the strength she needed to cope with the stress of becoming a single parent.

The social, cultural, economic, education, and medical factors in any family will determine how its members interact to help during a crisis. Major events—such as death of a spouse, jail term, loss of a job, or divorce—can be handled smoothly by some families, while more minor stresses—a change in social activities, a vacation, or a change in eating habits—may precipitate a crisis among others.

The mere absence of a family member who usually provides strong emotional support can precipitate a crisis. Or sometimes a family may suffer a number of crises at once: within one week's time a teenager gets cut from the

---

[15] Howard J. Parad, Ed., *Crisis Intervention: Selected Readings* (New York: Family Service Association of America, 1976).

[16] Hafen, et al., *Prescriptions for Health,* pp. 34-35.

basketball team at school, a grade-schooler is hospitalized with an appendicitis attack, the husband is laid off at the plant, and the wife is in a rear-end car collision.

Generally, a family that has pride in its culture, is economically stable, has established sources for health care, and whose members are educated and free from disease is best able to withstand stress. Families that suffer from social isolation, cultural conflicts, economic depression or abnormal concern over financial matters, inappropriate education or training, medical deprivation, or major medical problems are more susceptible to crises.[17]

Coping Mechanisms

Each person is different in his or her ability to cope, and each person has his or her preferred way of dealing with stress. Some people are defensive—they try to escape from the problem. Others are offensive—they meet the problem head-on and gain satisfaction in conquering it. In the long run the offensive position is best for the individual, who can then learn from the problem solving and who can better meet a stress next time it occurs. Those who choose to escape may begin to lean on drugs, alcohol, or suicide if the stress is not resolved quickly enough.[18]

Economic Resources

In some cases the availability of money can act as a buffer against anxiety. A woman is secure in knowing that there is money enough in the bank to feed her family even if her husband does lose his job; a man realizes that his insurance will cover all the hospital bills incurred during his illness. Economic security creates time and space in which to consider options and make adjustments. On the other hand, a young couple faced with a large medical bill after the birth of their first child may learn early in their marriage to work together and rely on each other. Money and interpersonal relationships should bolster each other, not replace each other.

EFFECTING CHANGE IN CRISIS

The goal of psychological first aid—crisis intervention—is to help people begin quickly again to function normally on their own. Your role is to help—"How can I assist this person?"—not to analyze—"Why did this happen?" One of the most

---

[17]Smilkstein, "The Family in Trouble—How to Tell," pp. 19-24.

[18]*EMT—Advanced,* Prepublication Edition, DOT HS 501207, National Highway Traffic Safety Administration, p. 435.

important factors in psychological first aid is *urgency*. A person who is experiencing a crisis feels out of control, anxious, tense, and panicked; a delay in help could upset the person to the point of self-destruction.

In general you must present a sharp contrast to the person's panic. Approach him in a controlled, warm, reassuring way. If the person's emotional crisis is too intense for you to handle send for professional help, but never abandon the person. Don't overreact to whatever the person says or does. Reassure him that his need for help is legitimate and normal, not shameful or abnormal.

Try to *do* something. In many cases listening is helpful, but then follow it up with action. After listening to a young man's story about the fire that destroyed his apartment and its contents, act to help him find new housing and work to obtain new clothing for him.

Never make false assurances, but extend hope and confidence. Don't promise the person that everything will work out; instead, make a sincere offer of help.[19]

In addition to these general suggestions eleven actions will help you assist someone who is experiencing crisis.[20]

1. *Act quickly.* A person experiencing a crisis may be so overwhelmed that he may become self-destructive if he does not receive help immediately. Most crises are short-lived, and even long-term crises work themselves out in about six weeks, but your quick help can make the crisis less severe and can help protect the person from hurting himself.

To begin, help the person understand the crisis; many people have no idea that the crisis they are experiencing is even related to an event. Help the person form the link between his feelings of despair and an actual event in his immediate past. Show that you understand the person's feelings by asking him questions: "You appear to be a little nervous. Is something bothering you?" Acknowledge the person's feelings—"I can understand why you would be angry"—and encourage him to express his feelings of guilt, fear, anger, and anxiety. As he talks give him feedback; ask him to clarify things you don't understand—"Why did it bother you when Chris asked for the car?"

Once the person is expressing himself well, help him explore the alternatives for dealing with the crisis; help him remember what he has done in the past in similar situations. As you talk about attempts to solve the crisis ask, "What else could you have done in this situation?"

Lead the person to his support system; he may not have considered talking

---

[19] *Comprehensive Emergency Services Training Guide,* p. 19.

[20] *Crisis Intervention.* p. 7; *EMT—Advanced,* p. 438; Schulz, *Emergency Department Drug Abuse Treatment Technician's Booklet,* pp. 68-70; *Comprehensive Emergency Services Training Guide,* p. 19; Hafen, et al., *Prescriptions for Health,* p. 36; Douglas A. Puryear, *Helping People in Crisis* (San Francisco: Jossey-Bass Publishers, 1979), pp. 186-87.

to his mother, his priest, his best friend. You might help the person by offering to call a member of his family, his minister, the police, or a friend. Maybe you could offer to drive him to a hospital if he has been injured, and you could arrange for someone to stay with his children if that is necessary.

2. *Control the environment.*   A person in crisis will perceive the environment as one of chaos and confusion, something impossible to manage. Take immediate steps to change the environment to one that is less threatening, more calm. Move the person to a quiet area, away from noise and onlookers; by this simple step you can often reduce the problem to one that is within the person's scope.

If the person doesn't seem to know you identify yourself immediately: "I'm your neighbor, Alice; I live in the yellow house on the corner, and I want to help you now." Identify the problem, and let the person know that you understand and are there to help. Unless the person has been seriously injured physically, wait to call an ambulance or to drive the person to the hospital; rushing him off to a hospital will only confirm his fears that something is terribly wrong. Talk to him wherever you find him—in his living room, in the grocery store parking lot, in his backyard—and ask other relatives or friends to leave for a few minutes while you talk to the person alone. Too many people will intimidate the person, and he will feel compelled to maintain control rather than letting his feelings out; one-on-one discussion at this point is most beneficial.

3. *Assess the person.*   Look at the situation carefully; assess what the person is telling you as it compares to the situation as you see it. Remember, the person's perception is what triggers crisis. You may think that a man is reacting beyond rationality after some neighborhood children pluck the heads off his roses; what you may not see immediately is that the man learned that morning of his wife's terminal cancer.

Assess the person's general alertness and ability to communicate by asking him questions that force him to respond. As you talk to him try to identify the cause of the crisis by asking open-ended questions that call for answers: "What's happened to make you so upset?" "Why are you away from home?" "Have you recently lost someone?" "Is there a reason you need help right now?" Watch the person's posture, body movements, eye glances, and mannerisms. Note whether the person is disheveled, intoxicated, distracted, forgetful, abnormally depressed or euphoric, or worried.

4. *Do something quickly.*   When a person is experiencing a crisis things need to happen right away for him to begin resolving the crisis. People in crisis tend to flounder; you need to move them toward meaningful, purposeful, coordinated, goal-directed behavior. The person needs to know that something is being done by him and for him. A mother who is distraught because her child has been injured in an accident in a distant town, for instance, can find some resolution in making arrangements to buy a bus ticket so she can be with him there.

5. *Set a limited goal.*   Part of resolving a crisis lies in the fact that the person can once again achieve some balance in his life. As a first step help the person achieve a limited goal; make it something that will challenge, but not overwhelm him. A person who is suffering a crisis after the death of a spouse may achieve a goal of collecting keepsakes and storing them in a safe place for their children to cherish in the future.

6. *Foster hope and expectations.*   People in crisis feel hopeless, and one of the best ways to help restore hope to a person in crisis is to clearly express expectations of him. Plan with the person in crisis; help him set some goals. This helps restore the person's self-esteem.

7. *Assess the person's support system.*   Find out what kinds of external resources the person has—school, church, friends, family members—and whether he is using them to help him overcome the situation. Find out how he has reacted in the past when presented with a stressful environment; will past solutions work again? To utilize supports the person must be able to think relatively clearly, have control of some of his emotions, recognize that there are significant people who can help him, and want to help him regain control.

8. *Plan for the future.*   When you set goals with the person make sure you assign each a time frame; place limits on the achievement of each goal so that the individual clearly understands that certain things must be accomplished within a certain amount of time. Aim these goals toward the future, helping the person move forward.

9. *Promote a good self-image.*   Guilt and feelings of incapacity can lead to a poor self-image for those who are suffering a crisis. To promote a better self-image treat the person with courtesy and respect. Show interest in areas of the person's life that are not involved with the problem. Make sure that others are kind and treat the individual with respect, and let the person do as much for himself as he possibly can.

10. *Encourage self-reliance.*   A crisis can cause a person to revert to an earlier time in life that was less threatening, with the result that a competent, independent person can become unable to do things for himself. Find things that the person can successfully accomplish for himself, and urge him to do everything possible.

11. *Listen actively.*   To listen actively you need to use three ears: two to hear the verbal message and one to sense the underlying feelings and emotions. As you listen question occasionally by rewording what he is saying to demonstrate that you are interested and that you understand. You can't just sit back and passively listen; you need to question, repeat, and lend support as the person attempts to express emotions.

As you listen don't try to solve the person's problems for him—it is critical that he do that himself. Help him express even painful emotions, such as guilt, hatred, or fear; sometimes simply coming to terms with such feelings can help an individual place them in proper perspective and regain some control. Let the person cry or shout if necessary.

Help the person gain an understanding of the connection between a hazardous event and the current crisis. Much of the person's panic could be a result of confusion. Help the person confront the reality of the situation, and tell him that he need not accept the burden of change all at once—he can work at it gradually as he feels able to.

Encourage the individual to assume regular chores, and discourage the use of medication, which can block the person's ability to adapt and solve the problem. As you listen be prepared to list alternatives that the person may not have considered.

WORKING WITH CHILDREN IN CRISIS

While working with children in crisis involves many of the general principles listed above some differences can help spell success. Remember, too, that you cannot work with a child without his parents' or guardian's approval unless the child's life is actually endangered.

DEAL WITH ISSUES INDIRECTLY   Many children are uncomfortable with direct questioning or discussion. First, they often don't understand the importance of what you are asking, and second, they often don't have the skills to adequately express themselves. Try watching the child play, and watch how he interacts with others. Then get involved in a game, in storytelling, or in picture drawing to draw out the information you need. For instance, if you suspect that a child is having difficulty because of pressures from his family, you could ask the child to draw a picture of his family while he tells you about each of the family members.

GIVE THE CHILD FOOD, AND ALLOW HIM TO USE THE RESTROOM A child who is physically uncomfortable will not be able to react as well as one whose basic physical needs have been taken care of.

KEEP THE SESSION SHORT   A child's attention span is much shorter than an adult's, and he won't be able to listen or respond as well once his attention wanders.

DO NOT LIE   Unpleasant facts may be involved in the crisis, and you may be tempted to shield or protect the child from them. Whatever you do, don't lie. Gradually help the child adjust to things that are painful, but be honest; a child's imagination can work up all kinds of terrible things when adults cover up the facts. You should never tell a child something false that will later erode his trust in adults when he discovers the truth.

ENLIST THE COOPERATION OF OTHER ADULTS   Parents are important in helping the child solve his crisis, since the family unit works best together. By asking the parents to help you you will enable the child to express himself to his parents and will open the channel for the expression of emotions that will help the child resolve the crisis.

EXPRESS HONEST EMOTION IN FRONT OF CHILDREN   When a child sees an adult who is upset and fearful—and who may even cry—the child realizes that those emotions are permissible. While the adult must remain in control of the situation he should be honest about his emotions, allowing the child the same honesty.

PROTECT THE CHILD FROM NEGATIVE COMMENTS   It's important to watch children carefully because they are apt to take everything they hear literally. Two small children were injured and their parents were killed in an ice cream parlor fire; a relative, standing in the hall, remarked, "Well, that's what you get for eating ice cream!" Their doctor had to work patiently with the children to convince them that eating ice cream was not a cause of injury or death.

DON'T TAKE A CHILD'S REACTIONS PERSONALLY   A child, out of fear or anxiety, may lash out. This does not mean that he dislikes you or resents the help you are trying to give him.

SIGNS AND SYMPTOMS OF CRISIS

How can you tell when a person is actually experiencing a crisis? When is it time to begin psychological first aid measures?

There are no simple answers. The way a person reacts in any stressful situation depends entirely on the mechanisms he has used over the years to deal with stress. Some people get angry and irritable; others feel weak and unable to care for themselves. Some symptoms—emotional, behavioral, and physical—indicate psychological crisis; a person who has experienced a hazardous situation and who manifests some or most of these signs should be dealt with as if in a crisis.

Physical Signs and Symptoms

The physiological signs and symptoms of psychological crisis include:

- Change in appetite
- Headaches (usually chronic)
- Abdominal pain
- Loss of sexual drive
- Rapid breathing
- Rapid heartbeat
- Extreme muscle tension
- Nausea and diarrhea
- Weight gain
- Persistent insomnia (inability to fall asleep easily or to stay asleep through the night)
- Peptic ulcer
- Digestive upsets (including gastritis, duodenitis, colitis, spastic colon, or "nervous stomach")
- High blood pressure

Emotional Signs

A number of emotions, sometimes conflicting in the same person, can surface as a result of crisis. The person will usually experience erratic changes in feeling; most experience fear, anxiety, and confusion. Other emotional signs include:

- Nervousness
- Tension
- Fatigue
- Hostility
- Anger
- Depression
- Ambivalence
- Inability to make decisions
- Panic
- Weeping spells or constant outbursts of temper
- Irritability
- Guilt
- Paranoia

While you can't often tell a great deal about a person's emotions by simply looking you can obtain clues through what he says. A person who says, "I never felt this way before" is bewildered; a desperate person may say something like, "I've got to do something—I don't know what, though." A helpless feeling may be expressed as "I can't manage this myself"; the emotion of apathy may be expressed as "Nothing can help me. I'm in a zero situation."

Behavioral Signs

Watching how the person interacts with others can provide valuable clues about the presence of crisis. Some common behavioral signs include:

- Inability to concentrate
- Preoccupation with the past
- Slips of the tongue while speaking
- Denial
- Delusions and/or hallucinations
- Change in habits
- Demanding, clinging behavior
- Withdrawal from regular activity
- Excessive drinking
- Drug addiction (watch for needle marks on the skin)
- Frequent use of hallucinogenic drugs
- Criminal behavior
- Serious juvenile delinquency
- Sudden carelessness in dress in a usually well-groomed person
- Alcoholism

HELPING YOURSELF

So far, we've talked only about what you can do to help those around you. But there's a lot you can do to help yourself through stressful situations in your own life. Five major elements will enable you to meet crisis situations of your own with greater strength and determination.

1. *Stop complaining.* Remember, change and challenge are necessary parts of growth; no one is exempt from them. Complaining might attract attention and sympathy from others, but it stops you from making decisions and moving forward in a positive way.

2. *Stop dwelling on unfavorable circumstances.* It's easy to dwell on unpleasant thoughts—to rehash worries, fears, and mistakes. Replace this negative kind of daydreaming with activity: work in the garden, clean your house, sew a dress, play a game of volleyball, go for a walk. Do something for yourself that you enjoy.

3. *Face your troubles.* It's easy to run away, to avoid thinking about things that bother or frighten you. But in the long run avoiding your problems creates more tension because the problems never get solved. You're never able to move on. If your problems are too terrifying to contemplate at length try thinking about them for short periods of time, identifying what is bothering you and planning for solutions. Then move on to other activities until you feel you can think about your problems again. Gradually work to solve your problems.

4. *Do things to help you express your emotions.*   Writing, acting, singing, role-playing, and other activities may help you express your emotions fully. A good habit to develop is to write in a journal several times a week; sorting out your problems on paper makes them seem more real and more approachable.

5. *Engage in secret service to others.*   Regular service to others, especially to those you dislike, does more to alleviate depression and anxiety than any other activity. Giving of yourself to others removes your focus from your problems and gives you something constructive to do. Rake a neighbor's lawn while she is at work; sweep the snow from a friend's windshield before dawn on a crisp December morning; leave a plate of warm cookies on a co-worker's desk. With an honest effort you'll forget about yourself.

Crisis—the inability to deal with changes and losses—is a normal part of life, and no person is immune to it. Every person faces crisis at some point in life, and every person develops his or her own unique way of dealing with that crisis. By exercising the principles of psychological first aid you can hasten and improve the coping process for yourself and those around you.

DEATH AND DYING

Every member of the human race has certain things in common with every other member of the human race. We have differences in the color of our skin, the languages we speak, the foods we eat, the traditions we use to pronounce the marriage covenant, and the very personal ways we worship. But there are two things all of us share: each of us is born, and each of us dies.

Birth signifies new beginnings: the miraculous unfolding of a human soul, the embryo of countless dreams, the vision of hope in a bright future. The things we use to symbolize birth—the tender buds on a pussy willow branch, the kaleidoscope wings of a butterfly emerging from a dark cocoon, the cluster of violets under the old back porch—are beautiful, inspiring vestiges of all that is good in life. Birth makes us reverent and peaceful. We are eager for birth.

But we dread death. Too often it represents an ending, a finality, a cessation of all that is good. Death signifies a departure from a life, friends, family, and experiences that have made life rich.[1] We fear death; we dread its

[1] Kathy Charmaz, *The Social Reality of Death* (Reading, Mass.: Addison-Wesley Publishing Company, 1980), p. 68.

arrival in our own spheres of existence. We envision blackness, sorrow, cob-webbed tombstones marching across the dying grass of a weed-choked cemetery. We cling tenaciously to life, even when life's melody has struck its final chord and we need to experience that other universal part of living: dying.

There can be peace—even beauty—in dying, in putting the finishing touches on a life well lived, a life of rich experiences and full, happy days. Because death is often the culmination of painful or debilitating disease we wrongly assume that death, too, is painful. But death is a freedom from pain, a release from care and burden. It is a release from this life and the opportunity to move on to other yet unknown experiences.

We can learn to appreciate death, to dread its coming less, if we under-stand what happens during the dying process and if we come to terms with the ways that our bodies, our minds, and our spirits are affected as we experience death. And because death is common to the human race the effort to understand death is an effort to understand the human experience a little better, an effort to draw closer to those around us and those we will grow to know during the jour-ney of our lives.

What happens in death reflects what happens in everyday life. The issues we face in death do not reflect a difference in nature, but rather a difference in intensity and scope from those we face in life. Death can be met in the same manner as we meet life; it can be a peak experience or it can be a final trauma, depending on how we look at it. We can regard death as a consummation to be avoided at all costs, or we can regard it as a culmination and a triumph.

But how do our emotions control our insights? Of course, people who die suddenly—like the ninety-year-old woman who crumples to the ground as she shuffled across the soft grass on her way to get the morning mail, or the twenty-year-old who perishes in a head-on collision—do not have time to think about their death situation, to compose their thoughts, to become emotionally in-volved with this ultimate growth experience. But those people who learn that they will die sometime soon—like the forty-five-year-old victim of a brain tumor who learns that she will die within the year—have the marvelous opportunity of preparing for death in many ways, including the emotional.

EMOTIONAL STAGES OF DYING

A dying person goes through five stages which, in fact, are similar to those mani-fested by anyone who faces any kind of extreme loss: loss of youth, loss of health, loss of employment, loss of status, or loss of a loved one.[2]

---

[2] Summarized from Elisabeth Kubler-Ross, *On Death and Dying* (New York: Mac-millan Publishing Company, 1969). Copyright © 1969 by Elisabeth Kubler-Ross.

Denial

When a person is first told that he is going to die he reacts with shock and disbelief. He denies that this is happening to him; his denial stems partly from fear. In a very real sense he refuses to believe the news that he will die and that anything is wrong with him. Some people maintain such a denial for only a few seconds; in the most extreme cases the denial period may last as long as several months. But eventually the person conquers that denial. Something obviously *is* wrong—he may be suffering pain, he may be hospitalized or be taken to clinics regularly for extensive and uncomfortable treatments, and others don't treat him the same way; they feel ill at ease around him, and they don't know what to talk about. Some are obviously embarrassed. Eventually people accept the truth of the news regarding their illness and death although some few die too quickly to adjust emotionally, and some respond abnormally with signs of emotional or mental illness.

As a whole America is a death-denying society. We emphasize youth, beauty, and physical fitness; less than one-fourth of all Americans have wills, and many people refuse to discuss death openly. In addition America is a leader in the heroic effort to save lives; we commonly hospitalize even terminal patients and subject them to all kinds of experiments in an effort to prolong life. Many people feel that by denying death they can control it.[3]

Anger

Once a person works through the denial period and accepts the fact that he is going to die, he enters the second stage of reaction: anger. "Why me?" is a normal question—why didn't this terrible illness strike the man next door, the woman at the supermarket, or the mailman? This stage is characterized by bitterness; the person becomes difficult, nasty, and demanding. He often criticizes viciously the ones who are trying the hardest to help him. This stage is extremely difficult for both the dying person and those who surround him—loved ones, family members, and doctors and nurses.

A tremendous amount of anger is penned up in a dying person at this stage of reckoning; relief of this anger is essential, and it eventually comes. One person may need to take a drive in the car and scream until he is exhausted; another may simply need to discuss the problem with someone who understands.

Bargaining

Then the person enters the third stage: bargaining. Whether subconsciously or overtly, the person promises something in exchange for an extension of life; she

[3] "Death in America: No Longer a Hidden Subject," *U.S. News and World Report,* November 13, 1978, p. 68.

might promise to donate her kidneys or eyes, might start going to church every Sunday, or might patch up an old quarrel that has been causing unhappiness for years. But in this bargaining stage promises are rarely kept. For instance, a woman who begs to be kept alive just until her daughter finishes high school then wants to see her through college, see her son-in-law, hold her grandchild. This stage is earmarked by a frantic, desperate attempt to work something out, to make things better. The person feels for some reason that she can control the situation, can determine the course of the illness and postpone or prevent death by doing all kinds of things she's always considered "right." But eventually the realization comes. She does not have control over death.

Depression

Enter stage four: depression. This can be another difficult period for those who surround the dying person; it is difficult for us to tolerate grief and depression for long periods of time. In some patients who are terminally ill the stage of depression can last for months; it can linger on almost as long as it takes the person to die. Those of us who live grieve over something we have lost; the dying person must grieve over impending loss. And it might help us to understand and tolerate the dying person better if we realize the magnitude of his loss. Imagine how sad you would be if you lost someone who was very dear to you; you would mourn, and your sorrow would probably be quite intense. Imagine, then, the prospect that faces the dying person; he is going to lose not one, but *all* of the people who are dear to him—he is losing everyone he has ever loved. To help a person who is dying you must understand and respect that kind of loss and the courage it takes to face it.

As the dying person eventually learns to cope with this depression and sense of loss he finally begins to separate himself from those he knows he will lose. He asks to see people—his cousin, a friend at work, a favorite aunt—for the last time. And then he chooses one special person with whom he wants to spend a great deal of time. This is usually a spouse or, in the case of a child, a parent. He will choose a person whose companionship offers him comfort, peace, and warmth—someone who will sit and hold his hand and be near.

Acceptance

At this point the dying person has entered the final stage of emotional adjustment: acceptance. This is *not* resignation. Resignation means giving up, losing hope. No, it is not that; a dying person comes to terms with himself. He accepts his condition, but he is not defeated by it. His time is near, and he is all right. People who have come to this point have a great deal to teach us all about living and dying; their experience is one of growth for them and progression for those who are lucky enough to share in it. There is no more fear and anger; there is peace and hope for what is to come.

Remember that each person is an individual; for some, these stages may overlap. Each person will experience each stage for a different duration and with different intensity; it is not fair to compare the behavior of one dying person with the behavior of another. A knowledge of the stages of death can help you come to an understanding of death and of the emotions encountered by the dying person.

NEEDS OF THE DYING PERSON

Those of us who have not died are in a poor position to understand fully what it is like to die and what it is like to go through the various stages of the death experience. It may be hard for us to know what a dying person needs, how we can best help him through this time in his life. We do know that certain emotional and physical needs must be met, and with compassion and empathy you can provide a real service to those who are dying.

Any situation that is difficult to face, like death, is easier when undertaken in a supportive environment with the help of people who are knowledgeable. Because death is distasteful to so many the dying are sequestered away, avoided, and ignored in large part. Illness and disease make it necessary to hospitalize some, but too often the terminally ill are hospitalized or removed to nursing homes because of a family's inability to handle the emotional stress of the death. It takes courage to confront death squarely—to live night and day with a person who is creeping ever closer to that solemn finality. A key to being able to handle that stress is to come to an understanding of how the dying person feels.

Unfortunately, death is usually a time of fear; to help a dying person overcome fear you need to confront the vast network of needs the dying person has. Most of those needs can be fulfilled by concern and loving family members in the home. Eight major needs of the dying person follow.[4]

1. *The need to feel secure.* The dying person needs to feel that those who are caring for him are competent. If the dying person is in pain and requires medication you should ask a doctor or nurse to teach you how to administer the medication and then you should make sure you project an aura of confidence as you do so. Convey the same attitude of confidence in all the things you do for the person: helping him with a bedpan, taking his temperature, changing his dressings, or feeding him.

---

[4]Taken from Ned H. Cassem and Rege S. Stewart, "Management and Care of the Dying Patient," *International Journal of Psychiatry in Medicine,* 6, no. 1/2 (June 1975) 6-11.

2. *The need to feel that others are concerned about him.*   You need to overcome any revulsion you have toward death and toward the dying person and place yourself in his position instead. Spend time with him, talk to him; make sure he knows that *he* is as important to you as the daily routine of caring for him. It is especially important that dying people have the chance to talk about their situation, they need the chance to sort out their own feelings, too. A classic example was the forty-one-year-old sportsman who was dying from a particularly painful form of cancer; he had been an active, vital, energetic individual all of his life, and the cancer had riddled him with such excruciating pain that he was bedridden for the last several months of his life. Those who came to visit him, and there were many, attempted to cheer him up by discussing the weather, the happenings at work, the upcoming election—anything but his pitiful condition. About two weeks before his death he finally vented his frustrations to a small group of office colleagues as he asked, "Why doesn't anyone want to talk about *me?* I'm dying! I need to talk about why I can't skydive anymore, and what it's like to face death. Everyone comes in here and talks about everything but me. I need to know that you care about me and what I am feeling. Please don't ignore my situation."

If you are confronted with talking to a terminally ill person remember that the dying like to talk about things that make them more real, such as family, work, hobbies, interests, likes, dislikes, the past, and the present. The terminally ill also like to talk about themselves.

3. *The need to be comfortable.*   In most cases of terminal illness pain medication is essential. If you are responsible for administering it make sure that you administer proper dosages and that you administer it on time. Even five minutes can mean a world of difference to a person who is teetering on the edge of blinding pain.

There are many simple things you can do to make a dying person comfortable. If he is bedridden make sure that there is plenty of light and fresh air in the room. Try to understand how he feels: fluff his pillows occasionally, or get an extra blanket. Stay tuned in to the things he needs and wants. Even minor things like helping a bedfast person brush his teeth so that the taste in his mouth is fresh can greatly improve his outlook.

4. *The need to communicate.*   Let a dying person tell you his story. He might want to tell you about his life, relive parts of his life for you, or just talk about his condition. Be a good listener; make an effort to really understand what he is trying to say. And don't forget nonverbal communication. You can let a dying person know where he stands with you by a friendly pat on the arm, a touch of the hand, a wave, a wink, or a grin.

Some dying people don't *want* to talk about death. Respect that wish. In all of your communication with the dying remember the importance of dignity and self-respect.

5. *The need to be with his children.* If the dying person is at home make sure that the children have ample opportunity to spend time with him. If he is in the hospital discuss with the physician or nurse the possibility of allowing the children to come to the hospital for a visit. Remember, of course, not to force a child to visit against his will.

6. *The need for family togetherness.* It is critical that the dying person feel the support and concern of loved ones. Family members often take the opportunity at the time of death to fly from distant parts of the country so that they can attend the funeral. How much more important that they fly in *before* the death occurs so that they can spend time with the dying person. There they will have the chance to talk and to show love and concern; the dying person doesn't care how many family members show up at the funeral—he needs their support while he is dying. One busy accountant flew to Phoenix from Toronto three weeks before his brother died to spend a weekend; many of the family members protested, saying that death was not that near and that he would just have to return again for the funeral. "That's all right," he remarked, "John needs me now—not at the funeral."

If the dying person is at home family members should take every opportunity to be with him, both individually and as a group. Special care should also be taken to involve the dying person in the daily rounds of living as he dies. If he is in the hospital visits should be arranged as often as possible without draining the person of strength. It is especially important to the dying person to have family members with him at the time of death. If he is in a hospital make clear to the physician that you and other family members, if necessary, want to be with the patient at the time of death, and provide telephone numbers where you can be reached.

7. *The need for cheerfulness.* A dying person isn't dead yet, he still possesses the same wit and sense of humor he always had. Help him have fun.

8. *The need for consistency and perseverance.* Be constant; keep up your vigil with the same intensity until death has occurred. One twenty-six-year-old woman was mobbed with visitors when she was first hospitalized for the brain cancer that took her life; as her illness progressed, however, and she needed love and support even more, her visitors dwindled off until only a few made the effort to be with her regularly. A great fear of the dying is isolation—do all you can to alleviate that concern.

RIGHTS OF THE DYING PERSON

Along with certain needs the dying person also has important rights.

1. *The right to know the truth.* Some doctors, in an effort to protect the patient from grief, tell family members the truth about the patient's condition but tell the patient himself something different. A dying person has the right to know the whole truth about his condition; if the person expresses that desire encourage the doctor to be truthful with the patient. Remember, though, that some patients do not *want* to know the grim reality of their illness; these patients need not be told.

2. *The right to confidentiality and privacy.* It should be up to the dying person, not up to you or some other friend or family member, to tell others about his condition. He probably wants to keep some aspects of his illness quiet; respect that desire.

3. *The right to consent to treatment.* Any patient deserves to have a full explanation of proposed treatment and then to decide whether or not he wants the treatment. Some types of treatment, such as chemotherapy used in the treatment of cancer, bear unpleasant side effects. The dying person has the right to know ahead of time what these side effects are: that his hair will fall out, that he will experience double vision, that he will be nauseated most of the time. If he decides against the treatment it should not be administered. As a friend or family member, encourage the patient to get full information about his treatment, and let him know that he has the right to refuse anything he feels uncomfortable about.

4. *The right to choose the place to die.* Some people want to die at home, where friends and family members can be gathered. Others feel more comfortable in a hospital, where there are trained medical experts to lessen the pain. When at all possible the person's wishes should be honored. A person who wants to die at home can be sent home just before death, and family members can be instructed on how to carry out essential nursing procedures until death occurs.

5. *The right to choose the time of death.* Many states have recognized the right to choose time of death by instituting natural death acts and providing for living wills.

6. *The right to determine the disposition of the body.* If a dying person lets you know that he wants to be cremated instead of buried, honor that wish.[5]. If he wants his eyes to be donated to an eye bank see that it is done.

MEETING NEEDS OF THE DYING

Many things can be done at home or by members of the family at the hospital to meet the needs and guarantee the rights of the dying person.

[5] Arlene McGrory, *A Well Model Approach to the Care of the Dying Patient* (New York: McGraw-Hill Book Company, 1978), pp. 75-77.

HELP HIM MAINTAIN HIS DIGNITY UNTIL THE END   Such simple things as helping him stay modest while in bed, providing him with baths and opportunities to brush his teeth and shampoo his hair will help him feel more attractive and comfortable.

OFFER HIM HOPE   You may not necessarily offer hope that the dying person will be cured of his disease and live, but hope that in death he will experience marvelous things barred from those who are tied down by mortality. Remind him of his religious beliefs, if he has them, and help him explore the possibilities of life after death.

HELP HIM KNOW THAT HE IS STILL VALUABLE AND WORTHY OF SELF-ESTEEM   Even in the most outrageous stages of disease let the dying person do things for himself if it is at all possible. If you need to feed him let him hold the straw or spoon. If you need to bathe him let him bathe a small area of himself, even if it's only a few inefficient dabs. One dying man who could perform almost no physical task because of weakness and pain wanted to leave his children the legacy of his life; his wife helped him by turning off and on a cassette recorder and changing tapes when he felt strong enough to speak. He was able to record a brilliant oral history that his children still treasure. If nothing else let the dying person make simple decisions, such as what to eat for dinner.

LET HIM PARTICIPATE IN GIVING AND RECEIVING   Many dying people are concerned that loved ones inherit certain possessions. A writer who did not have a family was well known throughout her office for her deep love of music; she had often given concert tickets to colleagues or called others into her office if a beautiful passage of music was on the radio. A week before her death from cancer she asked her landlady to bring a cardboard box filled with her favorite stereo albums to the hospital. She spent hours thumbing through them, deciding which person in the office would most like which album. The day after she died the albums arrived at the office—a tattered box of carefully chosen albums, each one bearing the name of an office worker and each one stamped with the dead person's name. There was a comedy album for the office clown, a Beverly Sills album for the office opera buff. The thoughtfulness invested in the gesture helped everyone in the office and helped the dying person to feel joy in her ability to give.

LET HIM ACT OUT HIS FRUSTRATIONS AND ANGERS   Do not censure or ridicule. Frustration and anger are important to the dying person, and he needs to know that he will not be rejected if he honestly expresses his feelings.

ALLOW THE DYING PERSON TO HAVE PRIVACY WHEN HE NEEDS IT   Some dying people will want to be with someone at all times; others will need time alone to think and sort out their feelings. Schedule some times during the day when the dying person can be alone and when he will be uninterrupted by those outside the family.

TOUCH AND HOLD THE DYING PERSON   Often a person who is dying, especially one who is dying of a disfiguring disease, will be afraid that he is repulsive to others. One such woman instructed the hospital staff to bar all visitors from her room because her family had avoided physical contact with her, and she had convinced herself that she was aesthetically offensive to others. Her death was lonely and difficult because of this restriction. Physical contact is critical to the emotional well-being of the dying person. Smooth his hair, hold his hand, or, if he is in a great deal of pain, touch him lightly in some area of his body that will not hurt him. Some people ask to be held by loved ones as they die; you should not hesitate to do this for a loved one if he wants you to. At that point, fears of hurting the person—of jarring an intravenous tube loose, for instance— are groundless. The comfort of physical contact can provide peace and an overwhelming sense of well-being that compensates for any physical discomfort.

HELP THE DYING PERSON WORK OUT MATTERS OF CONCERN TO HIM   Some people, especially heads of households, will be concerned to see that everything is in order: that the will is properly executed, that the insurance papers are organized, and that the family they are leaving behind is well cared for. Persons who are bedfast will feel helpless and frustrated at their inability to take care of these matters by themselves; ask them if there are things they would like done, and if there are help them locate the papers they need to get things in order.

Forty-five-year-old Glenn had suffered for over three years with a rare form of cancer of the liver. He was able to continue to work until four months before his death. He was naturally concerned about his young wife, thirty-six years old at the time, and his two small children; he wanted some kind of assurance that their futures would be taken care of and that their lives would be richer for having known him. A thoughtful friend and colleague helped Glenn with financial planning during the three years he continued to work and helped him explore legal matters he hadn't known about previously. The Christmas before his July death he presented his wife with the deed to the house—he'd been able to pay the mortgage ten years early—the title to the car, and savings bonds for the two children to attend college. He died in peace, knowing that his family was taken care of and that financial worries would not plague them as a result of his death.

GIVE THE PERSON PERMISSION TO DIE   You let the dying person know whether he is expected to live or die by the way you treat him and by the way you act around him. Help him prevent feelings of guilt and depression by letting him know in your own way that you have accepted what he must do and that you love him just as deeply as before.

It is easier to accept the death of an elderly person than the death of a child. We tend to reflect that the elderly person lived a full, happy life with the chance to marry, bear children, and have a satisfying career; for a child, however, these things are cut short, and that fact seems to make coping with a child's death more difficult in many cases. The family and loved ones need to give the child the permission to die as fully as they would an older family member.

EXPLAINING DEATH TO CHILDREN

At some time in your life you will most likely need to describe death to a child—perhaps it will be your little girl, who sees her grandfather die slowly of a stroke, or your little boy, who loses a schoolmate to leukemia, or even a toddler whose kitten is run over by a car.

How do you explain death to a child? Chances are the child will have already heard about death from television, friends, or some other source—possibly even from overhearing an adult conversation. How you approach a child depends on his age and his level of development. A rough guide to a child's concept of death normally depends on his age.

From infancy, typically about six months of age, until about three years of age a child perceives death as an absence, a state of nonbeing. The major fear of a child in this age bracket is a fear of abandonment. A terminally ill child of this age will understand that his parents are leaving him, but not that he is the one who is doing the leaving.

From three to five years of age children are frightened by death because they see it as a mutilation, they associate bodily injury with death, probably because of the experience of seeing dead animals, most of whom are injured. Most children at this age also see death as a punishment, as something they caused. A four-year-old decides that his mother died because he wished she were dead, and a five-year-old thinks she is sick because she broke her mother's favorite crystal bowl. Death for these children is not as devastating as for children who are older, because these younger children think death is temporary; they think that, like the leaves on the trees, all things come back in the spring.

From five to seven years of age children still fear death, but for a different reason. While they are beginning to distinguish between death as a permanent condition and absence as a temporary condition most children at this age think that death is caused by ghosts, monsters, the bogeyman, or the angel of death— some personified, real being who is out to "get" them.

A more permanent, adult concept of death emerges in children from the ages of eight to eleven. Although he recognizes death as a biological event the child in this age group may still ask questions and express some underlying fears about mutilation, aloneness, or lack of safety. These fears are often expressed through symbolic wings or stories. Children at this age have a firm grasp of death as a permanent situation. Because a child at this stage is beginning to be influenced by religious training he often fears going to hell or some eternal place of punishment for the "bad" things he's done.

As children enter adolescence most have a complete and well-founded understanding of death. Most go through the normal stages of denial, anger, bargaining, depression, and acceptance, although to a lesser degree than do adults. A teenager who is dying needs to cope with the normal stresses of adolescence—establishment of a values system, emancipation from parents, establishment of a self-identity, and adjustment to the opposite sex—in addition to the stresses entailed in learning to die. At this age the child is especially concerned with losing self-control and becoming helpless; to most, death is a blow to the self-image and causes severe frustrations arising from feelings of being unfulfilled.

Considering the child's age and level of emotional development, you can approach death honestly and openly. Sincere and genuine communication with someone he trusts is critical to a child of any age who is concerned with death, whether it be his own or someone else's. Parents who try to stifle information do a double harm. First, they diminish the child's curiosity and therefore diminish the child's capacity for growth. Second, they leave the child to rely on his own imagination—which, depending on his age, is usually much more devastating than the truth. [6]

HELPING A CHILD FACE DEATH

Children approaching death go through various emotional stages during which their impressions and understanding vary widely. It is critical to help a child adjust to his own death;[7] a general rule is to tell the child the truth about his situation in terms simple enough for him to understand if he expresses the interest in knowing such information. A child who denies his condition and expresses no interest in knowing its eventual outcome should not be burdened with such information until he is ready for it.

[6] Barbara Lee Sheer, "Help for Parents in a Difficult Job—Broaching the Subject of Death," *American Journal of Maternal Child Nursing,* September/October 1977, p. 321.

[7] Andre D. Lascari, "The Dying Child and the Family," *Journal of Family Practice,* 6, no. 6, 1279-86; and Mark L. Held, "The Dying Child: The Importance of Understanding," *Medical Insight,* March 1974, pp. 13-17.

Even children who are told they are seriously ill may ask questions about treatments and hospital stays, but they fail to follow the line of questioning to its obvious end: what will happen to me when there are no more drugs available? Children have the enviable ability of surviving on hope and are often satisfied with the fact that there is even *one* more treatment available. It is normal and common for children to avoid doctors, nurses, parents who may strip them of hope.

Depending on the child's age and stage of development you will need to do specific things to prepare him for his own death.

PRESCHOOLERS   Children under school age do not really understand death; they equate it with a fear of being deserted. Preschoolers need careful nurturance and parental supervision during the dying process. A child who is undergoing extensive medical treatments will probably fear the treatments because they are unknown and he doesn't understand them. For such a child it is helpful to explain the procedure briefly in language he can understand and perhaps demonstrate the procedure first on a doll. Encourage the child to ask questions, and do your best to answer them; you may need to enlist your doctor's help in learning about specific procedures.

If your preschooler asks you, "Will I die?" you might point out that he will not die today or tomorrow. For children under the age of five it is difficult to conceptualize a sense of future, even two weeks away. He will be satisfied to know that he will not die today or tomorrow—time concepts he *can* grasp. Your answer will serve two important purposes: it will fulfill the child's need to deny his own death, and it will tell him truthfully what will happen today or tomorrow. Anticipation of death will probably not occur with a preschooler, since it is rare in a child before the age of five.

You will need to deal carefully with a preschooler who is seriously ill, because children under the age of five commonly associate their illness with some wrongdoing of their own. Help the child understand, if you can, that the illness has nothing to do with his behavior or thoughts. Children who live with this burden of guilt concerning their own illness react in a number of ways. Those who accept the guilt become passive and withdrawn; those who deny the guilt and refuse responsibility for the illness project responsibility onto others and become angry and rebellious. Some children direct intense anger at their parents, because the parents allowed them to become ill.

As death approaches you can convince the child through stories and careful conversation that death does *not* involve mutilation and that it is a peaceful and painless experience. Because preschoolers associate death with an absence of love and attention it is important that dying preschoolers not be left alone for significant amounts of time. If the illness requires that the child be hospitalized try to arrange to be with the child as often as possible. Ideally, a family member should be at the child's side around the clock so he will realize that he has not been deserted by those he loves.

AGES FIVE TO SEVEN During the early years in school children begin to understand that death is permanent, and most anxiety will be noticed immediately after you tell a child of this age that he is going to die. Even grade-school children have the emotional ability to face the prospect of death, and such a child must grieve before he dies.

Children of this age fear death with a stunning intensity, and most will ask point blank whether they are dying. The child really doesn't want to know if he's going to die, though—what he's asking is for an explanation of why he feels so ill and an assurance that he will be cared for. He needs help from his parents, family members, best friends, and classmates.

When a child of this age feels particularly ill he might timidly ask, "Am I ever going to get well?" or "Am I going to die?" You should explain that some children do die when they become very ill, but that many children recover from serious illnesses. You should tell them that his doctors and others are doing everything they can to help him get better. Tell children the truth—that some children die and some recover—but never extinguish their hope. Assure them that neither you nor their doctor will abandon them.

As a preschooler, a child between the ages of five and seven fears that he is ill as a punishment for something he did wrong. Tell him—by your words and your actions— that he is not responsible, that you love him, and that he is not being punished. Answer what questions the child asks, but don't delve into areas he has not quizzed you about.

AGES SEVEN TO TWELVE   Older children, who have begun to conceptualize religious teachings and who have a basic understanding of death and its permanency, need opportunities to discuss their thoughts and feelings with parents or other adults they trust. With children this age, as with those of younger ages, the main anxiety is that of separation. You should make every effort possible to reassure the child and to make sure that he is never left alone.

Some hospitals have adopted a policy of allowing a child to be taken home before death so that he can be surrounded by his family and the comfort of familiar surroundings at the time of death. Ask your doctor if your hospital will consider releasing the child immediately before death; most will unless medical conditions make a trip home impossible. Sometimes an older child will express a preference about where he wants to die; if at all possible his wishes should be granted.

ADOLESCENCE Dying is probably hardest on the adolescent, who can appreciate the meaning of death but who cannot accept the fact of his personal death. A critical issue in adolescence is the struggle to establish an individual identity and to gain independence from the family unit. At this crucial stage in life the adolescent now comes face-to-face with the prospect of developing an illness so severe that he becomes dependent again on his parents, a possibility that makes the death experience all the harder and increases his personal stress and frustration.

Adolescents are almost always resentful and angry when faced with a terminal illness. Older adolescents can usually overcome this resentment and anger so they are able to accept treatment and grieving. However, many younger adolescents cannot overcome this resentment and anger; they may be fiercely independent to the end.

The adolescent is also worried about being "different," about deviating from the norm established by members of his peer group. Imagine the humiliation and the loss of self-esteem suffered by the teenager who can no longer participate in group activities, who has to go to bed early in the evening because of devastating weakness, or who becomes disfigured as a result of disease. The identity and image the adolescent has worked so hard to achieve can be thrown out of kilter as his friends abandon him at this difficult point in his life.

Much like the younger child, the adolescent suffers deep guilt and believes that he is somehow responsible for his demise. Because of this guilt, and because of his struggle for independence, he is likely to reject the offers of support and help from members of his family, he sees them as a threat to his pride. Sadly, death for the adolescent can be a very lonely experience, wrought with frustration and grief at being so imperfect that he has not been able to fulfill his goals and dreams.

Most adolescents detest dishonesty, and if a teenager asks for the facts he should be told. Listen to his questions; he will be telling you what kinds of answers he wants. If he indicates to you by his speech and actions that he absolutely needs to deny completely the prospect of his own death, support that denial. For reasons of emotional health he should not be obligated to face unbearable realities that he cannot tolerate. If he asks, "I'm not going to die, am I?" he is obviously begging you to support his denial. You can answer, "Not right now." If he is strong enough to handle more information he may ask you how long he will live. Answer him truthfully, but give him hope: "Your doctor says that you will live about three more months, but many patients who have your same illness die in three to six months, and many more live longer." If he does not ask you when he is going to die you can assume that he is not ready to receive that information; don't give it to him.

If a child has a terminal disease never give false hope to his brothers and sisters. Usually a child over the age of three will know that something happened. Even children who are too young to understand need special attention and support; most children under the age of three who lose a brother or sister will fear for their own safety and security, even if the concept of death is not fully understood. Spend extra time with the child, and offer tokens of security—bedtime stories, a soft doll or teddy bear, willingness to hold and cuddle the child.

You need to help the children prepare for the death and to deal honestly with it. You can maintain a delicate balance between offering false hope and not dashing hope altogether. You might say something like, "Yes, John is very sick, and many people die from the disease that John has. However, sometimes doctors are able to make people with this disease well again. We will know better in a few months."

Reassure other children in the family that they will not "catch" the disease that killed their brother or sister. For instance, if a seven-year-old child is dying of leukemia and his five-year-old brother comes down with the mumps you might say something like, "Gee, Sam, you are the first person in this family to have the mumps," or, "Sam, you are really special. David (the dying child) never had the mumps," or, "The mumps! Those really hurt, but you'll be better in a couple of weeks. Then you can get out of bed and be completely normal again."

Reassure other children in the family that everything was done for the dead child. Let them know that you and the doctors did everything you could to keep the child out of pain and that every effort was made to help him get better.

If a child in the family is dying try not to treat him too differently than the other children. Siblings may resent a child who suddenly commands all the attention and care. Try to take family trips—including all the children, even the dying one—and involve everyone equally. Let siblings participate in the care of the child who is dying when it becomes necessary to care for him in special ways. A brother or sister could help feed a dying child, bring him a favorite toy, or wash his face for him. This helps a sibling feel involved, helps reduce his guilt over the death, and helps prevent feelings of rivalry and jealousy.

Once the child dies you will undoubtedly feel sadness, but you will probably feel a sense of relief for the child if you have been able to accept the fact of death and have had time to progress through the normal grief process, which is similar to the five stages dying persons go through. Other members of the family who have been able to accept the death will feel the same sense of relief; such feelings are completely normal. In cases of severe illness where the child suffered excruciating pain it is even normal to feel joy at the death. Those family members who have continued to deny the death during the child's illness, however, will feel the impact of the loss all at once and will have a more difficult time dealing with the grief.

In any death situation it is important to do all that you can to meet the needs of the dying person and to assure the best possible environment in which he will spend the final days of his life.

Remember, because they have progressed through the stages of grief with varying degrees of effectiveness, family members will react to the death in different ways; understand that these reactions are normal, and give each family member noncritical acceptance for his feelings.

GRIEF
AND MOURNING

All of us, at one time or another, experience loss in our lives: loss of a loved one, loss of a valued job, loss of priceless personal belongings. Such losses disrupt our lives; death, the loss of a loved one, reminds us abruptly of our own mortality and introduces the possibility of our own death.

Loss affects almost every facet of our lives. Long-standing habits are reversed. We feel abandoned; we experience despair, guilt, even anger. Almost always we feel an overwhelming emptiness.[1]

Probably the most devastating form of loss is the death of a loved one. Death is a familiar occurrence: most have seen it at close quarters by the time they reach the age of twenty. And because of our unique philosophies, religions, and personal beliefs, death involves much more than just the body's failure to function. Death involves a whole mass of beliefs, of attitudes, of emotions; sur-

[1] Edwin S. Schneidman, "Postvention: The Care of the Bereaved," unpublished manuscript in the possession of Brent Q. Hafen, p. 1.

vivors may feel responsibility for the corpse, may wear different clothes, may continue paying respect until their own deaths, as the Sicilians do.[2]

Grief and mourning are the processes by which we cope with loss, especially death. Grief and mourning in themselves are not considered a disease; only when a victim begins to suffer abnormal grief can the process be classified as a disease.

NORMAL GRIEF REACTIONS

Normal grieving is a process of healing—if one doesn't grieve, the loss won't be completely healed. And for growth to take place healing must occur. A victim of grief experiences five phases if he is experiencing a universal reaction, one that is healthy and normal and that eventually leads to healing and cessation of mourning. Those five phases are denial, awareness, restitution, resolution, and idealization.

Denial

The initial normal reaction to loss is denial—shock and disbelief, stunned refusal to believe that the loss has occurred. The victim in this phase simply refuses to accept or comprehend what has happened; he often becomes numb, tells himself the event *couldn't* have happened. Sometimes a victim may accept the fact intellectually, while emotionally he still denies it, such an individual won't react emotionally in any way that conveys knowledge of the loss. Some may try to carry out normal activities as though nothing has happened. Others may become dazed and may sit completely motionless, unable to move.[3]

The numbness that victims experience during this stage of grief enables them to attend to the necessary arrangements after the loss of a loved one. For most the period of disbelief or denial is short, lasting from a few minutes to a few days. When the period of denial lasts longer than a few days it is a signal that something is wrong. Some people need a sedative to sleep at night, but it's important that they not take a sedative during the day; such a daytime sedative can induce artificial calmness and can delay the normal process of grieving.[4]

Awareness

The shock and disbelief period is usually short; following that period of denial the individual usually develops a sense of awareness in which he emotionally

---

[2]Barbara Littlewood, "Interpreting Death," source unknown.

[3]Annete Edwards, Pamela Hay, and Lois Thompson, "Grief and Mourning," unpublished manuscript in the possession of Brent Q. Hafen, p. 269.

[4]Brent Q. Hafen, "Grief and Mourning," unpublished manuscript in the possession of author, p. 11.

acknowledges the loss. The reality of the loss—and, often, its implications—begins to penetrate the consciousness of the individual. At this point the victim will begin to feel the anguish and emptiness of the loss. In essence, the loss is no longer simply a part of the surroundings; the loss is a very real part of himself.[5]

During this phase the individual begins to experience emotion toward the loss. Anger is commonly expressed, especially if the individual feels that a person or institution was to blame for the loss. Some individuals even strike out in anger against a nurse or doctor who treated the dead loved one.

Some may blame themselves instead and may try to harm themselves because of extreme guilt. Others may act on impulse and may harm themselves quite unintentionally—such as a victim who pounds on her chest, thrusts his fist through a window, or drives irrationally and gets in an accident. During this stage the most anguish is felt; the expression of the anguish depends on what the culture expects of the individual. Several specific behaviors are common. Crying is a typical reaction; it indicates both deep remorse at the loss and regression to a helpless childlike state. During this stage the individual usually experiences tearful longing for the deceased or the lost object. Some may cry inwardly while not crying outwardly; others may not be able to cry at all, a problem that interferes with the normal grief process.

Emotions and reactions expressed during this stage may be triggered by a number of incidents, such as a friend's comment or a place associated with the loss. The woman whose husband died during the Christmas season is likely to feel some grief when she sees Christmas decorations or hears Christmas music as long as she remains in this second stage of grief. This stage of awareness usually peaks between two and four weeks after the death or loss and begins to subside after three months, but it may last up to one year.

Expressions of grief during this stage tend to be especially tense and painful during the nighttime hours, when the activities and distractions of the daytime are not present. In the case of loss of a loved one there is often preoccupation with the memory of the individual. Some victims even experience visual images of the dead person; for some these are an anxious and fearful experience, and for others a comforting experience. Blocking these images and memories interferes with the so-called good-bye to the deceased and limit the bereaved's capacity to return attention to the world of the living.

During this stage it is important that the grieving individual feel free to express his emotions; too often well-meaning friends and relatives encourage the individual not to cry, not to concentrate on the death or loss, not to think about the problem. On the contrary, the bereaved needs to give full expression to the emotions so he can have a chance to heal and to move on to other, more constructive emotions.

Some people get physically ill during the second stage of mourning; com-

---

[5] Information in this section is adapted from Edwards, et al., "Grief and Mourning"; and Hafen, "Grief and Mourning."

mon symptoms at this stage include digestive difficulties, poor appetite, weight loss, inability to sleep, and loss of sex drive. Women often experience menstrual difficulties. The elderly often appear to be grieving less than normal, but they show more physical symptoms of illness than others. Many people become irritable, restless, and unable to concentrate on ordinary tasks. Again, nighttime sedatives may be needed to help these people sleep, but tranquilizers should not be taken during the day.

The most important and effective treatment during this phase is the support and understanding of loved ones. The grieving person should be encouraged to express his emotions and should be told that those emotions and their accompanying physical symptoms are normal. The person should be helped to make cultural and religious adjustments if those are indicated.

Restitution

During the restitution phase the individual is helped more clearly to see the reality of the loss. In the death of a loved one, for instance, the victim has a chance to view the body, participate in a funeral, and see the casket lowered into the grave. Far from being a disturbing sequence of events, these often take place while the victim is in the company of friends and loved ones who can help him to cope better with the loss.

It is critical that the individual be allowed the expression of religious practices or cultural or social customs, especially in the case of death, no matter how strange those customs may seem to others. Such customs and practices reveal an important and necessary identity between the mourner and the dead.

Resolution

During resolution, the fourth stage of grief, the individual accepts the loss or the death and begins to pick up the threads of his life. He begins to visualize, for the first time, the possibility of functioning well without the spouse, job, money, or whatever he has lost. This stage, a stage of resolving the loss and reorganizing life to accommodate the changes, should be completed within one year after the loss.

As a first method of dealing with the loss the individual begins to resolve the emptiness within that the loss created. The individual progressively regains interest in the ordinary activities of life; at first memories of the loss or of the dead person will be painful and will evoke emotional reactions. Eventually, the individual will be able to remember the dead person with pleasure and interest and will be able to accept a new love object.

During this fourth phase of mourning the individual usually suffers various physical sensations, sometimes identical to a symptom suffered by the deceased person. This is especially common when a loved one dies of a long terminal illness. These symptoms, a way for the mourner to suffer on behalf of the deceased person and thereby ease his guilt toward the deceased person, usually last a brief time.

For a long time during this phase the mourner will seem completely preoccupied with thoughts of the deceased person. He will place a great deal of emphasis on the person who died, and will want to bring up, talk about, and think over memories of the dead person. At times this becomes a long and painful process. It continues until the mourner has developed an image of the deceased that is almost devoid of negative or undesirable traits.

The mourner's religious belief—particularly beliefs about whether he will meet the deceased person after his life—will play a big part in how he is able to resolve the loss.

Idealization

The fifth and final stage of mourning involves idealization, repression of all negative and hostile feelings toward the deceased. There is a disadvantage to this repression; the victim often experiences fluctuating guilt feelings that may lead to fear and that often involve regret for past acts or fantasies of inconsiderateness, unkindness, or hostility toward the deceased.

But two important things are achieved by idealization. First, the recurring thoughts and memories help the individual to create a vivid image of the deceased, the person then does not seem quite so lost. Second, the individual is able to remember, and eventually to concentrate on, the more positive aspects of the relationship with the deceased.

In some cases a mourner who has lost a loved one may unconsciously or consciously take upon himself certain admired qualities and attributes of the dead person. Some adopt mannerisms, others voice the desire to carry on the deceased person's good deeds and ideals. If the individual is suffering from extreme guilt he may assume undesirable traits of the deceased or may even assume symptoms of the deceased; some excessively guilty individuals exaggerate the need to fulfill the wishes of the deceased.

During this final stage the reminders of the dead person or loss evoke fewer feelings of sadness, and feelings of hostility or anger toward the dead person can be tolerated with much less guilt. As the ties are progressively loosed the earlier yearnings for the lost person begin to be replaced by a returning to life and reality.

The successful process of mourning usually requires a year or longer. Those who are able comfortably and realistically to remember both the pleasures and the disappointments of the lost relationship have healed most successfully. The healing process requires a great deal of support and comfort during the first stages and relatively little assistance or support during the final stages. During even the final stage, however, it is not uncommon for the individual to experience brief recurrences of grief and feelings of loss; as in the earlier stages, the victim should be encouraged to express his feelings openly.

Seven major features are common in almost all grieving people.[6]

1. A process of realization, moving from denial of the loss to a resolution and acceptance of the loss.
2. A feeling of anxiety and fear.
3. An urge to search for and find the lost person, sometimes in some other form.
4. Anger and guilt. This includes severe outbursts toward those who try to help the bereaved person accept the loss.
5. Feelings about and fear of internal loss or mutilation.
6. Adoption of the symptoms, mannerisms, or traits of the dead person; lack of a sense of presence within the self.
7. Abnormal variations of the normal grief process. Among the most common are simply excessive or prolonged expressions of grief.

ANTICIPATORY GRIEF

The process of anticipatory grief—grieving over a loss that you anticipate, such as death of a loved one from an extended illness—can be less severe than grief following a sudden, unexpected death, because most of the grief is completed before the death actually occurs. There are four stages of grief in the anticipatory grief process:[7]

1. *Depression.* Unlike the depression that may immediately follow an unexpected death, the depression in anticipatory grief comes with diagnosis, upon learning that the loved one will die. Those who are depressed before the death will still be upset after the death. In fact, it is generally true that those who are the most upset by the patient's illness will be the most upset by his death. However, the depression is unique to anticipatory grief work.

2. *Heightened concern for the ill person.* Following a sudden, unexpected death, many family members experience crippling guilt—for arguments that went unsolved, for not showing enough love toward the dead person while he was living, for not being an adequate spouse, and so on. In anticipatory grief a great deal of this guilt can be eliminated because the family members learn ahead of

---

[6]Milton Greenblatt, "The Grieving Spouse," *American Journal of Psychiatry*, 135, no. 1 (January 1978), 44.

[7]Richard Schulz, *The Psychology of Death, Dying, and Bereavement* (Reading, Mass.: Addison-Wesley Publishing Company, 1978), pp. 140-41.

time about the patient's illness and then have the chance over a period of months or years to show increased concern, love, and attention for the patient. They have the chance to make sacrifices for the ill person, which also helps assuage guilt. They have time to patch up arguments, finish personal business, and make up for lost time in the relationship.

3. *Rehearsal of the death.* During the time of illness the family members no doubt rehearse in their minds what they will do when the patient dies. How they will feel, how they will gain comfort, what actions they will take. Some make funeral plans months ahead, arranging for special musical numbers or arranging to grant the patient's wishes for his own funeral. Predictably, the stress of the loss is not as great on those who have already planned what they will do and who are, somehow, prepared for the death to take place.

4. *Adjustments to consequences of the death.* During the adjustment stage anticipatory grief work comes to a close. The survivors adjust to life without the dead person, unhook themselves from the past, and learn to make new acquaintances and to establish new relationships.

ABNORMAL GRIEF

Sometimes the grieving process gets bottled up. Occasionally something—guilt, well-meaning friends, social pressures—blocks the process of normal grief, and mourners are not able to heal properly following a death or other significant loss. Other times the mourners may not seem to grieve at all. In truth, they are not mourners, they are simply survivors. When grief seems abnormally prolonged, when a person does not seem to grieve, or when a person becomes physically or emotionally ill as a result of loss, you should help the person seek professional help.

WHAT YOU CAN DO TO HELP

There are three general ways you can help anyone, regardless of age, to better cope with grief.

1. Help the person face the full reality of what has happened. You should help the person realize that the pain he feels is healthy and that this pain will eventually give way to healing.

2. Help the person know that he must break the bonds he once had with the

person who has died. In other words he needs to "withdraw" some of the emotional strength he has stored from the past to help him move on now.[8]

3. Help the person find new interests, satisfactions, and creative activities that will carry him for the rest of his life. This also includes helping him form new relationhips, meet new people, and face new challenges.[9] For example, you might have noticed an undeveloped poetic flare in a woman who has just lost her husband in a tragic accident. Encourage her to develop her talent; the writing of her poetry can help her express her feelings, will give her a hobby for life, and by encouraging her to associate with others in poetry groups will give her the opportunity to meet new people.

BEREAVED CHILDREN

Children usually grieve because of the loss of a loved one; they don't experience the other losses that adults experience, such as loss of employment, loss of power, loss of status, and so on. Children comprehend death in different ways depending on their age and on their emotional development, and some researchers think that children do not go through the same mourning process as adults do until they reach adolescence.[10] They proceed more slowly than adults do, and their grief process usually takes a longer time than that of adults.

A child has two problems: first he needs to grasp the concept that death is permanent—that a dead person will *not* be coming back—and then he must be able to release the strong emotional ties he had with the person. This is especially difficult if the child was extremely dependent on the person; perhaps it was his mother, a grandmother he relied on heavily, or a brother he was very close to.

The loss of a loved one, especially a parent, is different for a child than for an adult. Adults generally have several meaningful relationships, and they distribute their love and interests accordingly—usually among spouse, parents, friends, colleagues, work, hobbies, and other activities. A child, on the other hand, invests almost all of his feelings in his parents, concentrating on a single relationship that is rich and intense. When this relationship is terminated through death the loss can be devastating.[11]

---

[8] Edgar N. Jackson, "Grief," in Earl A. Grollman, ed., *Concerning Death: A Practical Guide for the Living* (Boston: Beacon Press, 1974), p. 9.

[9] Ibid.

[10] Anne S. Watt, "Helping Children to Mourn, Part I," *Medical Insight*, July 1971, p. 32.

[11] Erna Furman, *A Child's Parent Dies* (New Haven, Conn.: Yale University Press, 1974), p. 12.

How Do Children Mourn?

Generally, any child over the age of two will need help in understanding what death means. For children the denial process is usually longer and more intense than for adults; the younger the child, the harder he will probably try to deny it. A child who is over the age of five may harbor fantasies about the return of the dead person for up to a week; children under five may do so for much longer. During this period the child might carry on as if nothing had happened. One little six-year-old boy was happy and carefree for several weeks after his mother died of a prolonged illness; finally his father noticed that he was sitting alone at times, staring blankly into space. This gave his father the opportunity to approach the child with, "I know how you feel when you think about Mommy. I feel that way, too. We probably will be sad for a long time."[12]

It will be hard for the child to accept the death all at once; a child can only stand a little pain at a time. He will probably realize and come to terms with one thing at a time. A four-year-old girl whose mother had died realized first that she wouldn't be there to tuck her in at night and realized later that she wouldn't be there to bake a cake. A seven-year-old boy whose mother was killed in an automobile accident told his father, "You will have to do the cooking now." It wasn't for several weeks that he finally accepted what had happened fully; he remembered that his little dog, Cocoa, had died and that he had never come back. The boy confronted his father with: "When Cocoa died he never came back again. Will Mommy ever come back?" At this point the child has probably worked things out in his mind and is ready to move on in the grieving process. Again, this takes much longer in a child than in an adult.

Because a child can only stand a little pain at a time you might be frustrated in your efforts to explain what has happened. Before he has accepted the death and before he has come to terms with what it means to him he will probably change the subject quickly when you try to talk to him about it, and he will probably not be able to listen to discussions about the death. You will need to approach him slowly, and you will need to gear your discussions to his own rate of mourning.

Once a child has accepted the loss he will probably begin to "act out" scenes in which he remembers the loved one. This ability to act out is a marvelous gift; it is unfortunate that adults don't do the same thing, because in the period following acceptance it helps a person adjust to the loss. The child will probably remember only happy, good episodes at first; he will usually block out painful or unhappy memories for some time. It is usually months, even years, before a child can bear the pain of remembering unhappy times with the loved one.

[12] Adapted from Watt, "Helping Children to Mourn," pp. 32-33.

As a child moves on in his mourning process it is extremely important that his needs be met so that he can be relieved of the fears that those needs will *not* be met. Basic emotional satisfaction is foremost among those needs, and you may need to reassure the child that those needs that the dead person fulfilled will still be taken care of. The younger the child is the more he probably needs a substitute close by. For instance, a young child who has lost a parent needs to have relatives nearby who can serve as mother or father substitutes for a while. A loving grandfather or aunt can help feed, clothe, and cuddle the child. Any child who has lost a loved one needs a warm, reliable person to comfort him and to fulfill his basic emotional needs; once those emotional needs are met it will be much easier for the child to accept the loss.

Guilt plays a much stronger role in a child's mourning than an adult's. For instance, a child may convince himself that his mother died because he was mad at her and wished she was dead once following an argument they had. Or he may decide that his father died because of something he, the child, did; a child often thinks that death is a punishment for some wrong deed. A rebellious seven-year-old may think that his own rebellion and misbehavior caused the death of his five-year-old sister. You need to help the child at every opportunity to realize that death happens independent of anyone's behavior and that he was in no way responsible for the death or illness.

Try to understand how a child might feel. One three-year-old resented a sick baby in the family because the baby commanded most of the parents' attention and care; the three-year-old often wished that the baby was dead so that she could command a little of the parents' attention and so that she could be the object of their concern. When the baby did finally die after more than a year of demanding the complete care and attention of the family, the little girl felt intensely guilty and responsible for the death. Her parents were wise enough to understand both the feelings of resentment for the sick baby and the feelings of guilt for the death. They were able to talk to the little girl; they approached the situation with something like: "We know that you had some bad feelings about our baby. We did, too, because it was hard to care for him all the time. We are glad that he died, because he is out of pain and he doesn't have to suffer any more. Now our family can spend more time together." Such a discourse may help a child realize that she was not the only one with resentful feelings and may help soothe her guilt.

Like guilt, the despair a child experiences is often more intense than that an adult experiences, and it may be expressed in a number of different ways. Some children choose to retreat completely from the world; others become hostile and rebellious. Still others express outright anger, especially against those family members who remain. A six-year-old, for instance, may hate his father for "letting" his mother die and may express hatred and anger against the father for "letting this happen to me." In such a case you should try to accept the child's angry feelings and help him realize that it is *normal* to feel angry. By doing this you will help steer him away from any more guilt he may experience. You might say something like: "I know you are mad that Mommy died. I'm mad, too. I wish we could find somebody to blame for her death."

Despair and sadness can be expressed in other ways, too. A child may regress to behavior indicative of a lesser emotional level, such as thumb sucking or wetting the bed. Or a little boy might suddenly refuse to play baseball, his dead father's favorite sport. Another child, in contrast, might assume the duties of her dead mother and might try to clean, cook, or do laundry. Another might simply refuse to talk about the dead person. Still another might develop imaginary ailments.

HOW TO HELP A BEREAVED CHILD

There are many ways that you can help a child who is in a process of mourning once you understand the feelings and emotions he may be experiencing. Any of the following, or combination of them, can help you support and comfort a child who has experienced the loss of a loved one.[13]

Allow the child to experience loss in small ways before he is confronted with the major loss of a loved one. A good way is to let him experience the death of a pet. Try buying a short-lived animal that your child can learn about, such as a goldfish. When the fish dies explain to the child what has happened, and try to help him understand the loss. Answer any questions honestly and openly. Make sure you wait an appropriate length of time before you replace the fish; the child needs to undergo a normal grieving period, and he needs to understand that the death of the fish is permanent—too quick a replacement might lead the child to think that the fish has "come back." You can further help the child distinguish between his new fish and the old one by getting a new fish that is distinct from the first one—a different color, different size, and so on—so that the child doesn't confuse it with the first fish.

While letting a child experience the death of a pet will not lessen his actual mourning if a parent dies it will help him understand death and will help him deal better with his sadness. You can draw a parallel between the two: "Your fish is dead, Kim. It can't feel anything any more, and it can't swim in its bowl. Burying your fish in the ground is one way of keeping it safe from other animals and from insects; your fish will be safe and warm in the ground. Our mommy is like this fish; she might die soon, too, because the doctor hasn't found a way to make her well. When that happens we will bury her in the ground, too, because she will be safe there. She won't hurt any more; she won't be able to feel anything. She will be happy." Advance warning of this kind will help a child begin

---

[13] Morris A. Wessel, "A Death in the Family: The Impact on Children," *Journal of the American Medical Association,* 234, no. 8 (November 24, 1975), 865.

his grieving process and will afford him the opportunity of asking any questions he needs to.

A number of good books on death have been written specifically for children; there are excellent ones for each age group. When your child is too young to read by himself read to him. Stop often during the story to let the child ask questions. When your child gets old enough to read by himself provide books that you have carefully reviewed. Let the child understand that you are available for questions at any time he feels he needs to ask them.

When the death of a family member is imminent it is important that the child be included in the dying process and included as a member of the family unit afterward. Explain fully to the child what is happening; don't try to hide the course of events. Depending on his age the child may need some simple medical explanations; make sure he is able to get answers to questions that are bothering him. If the child expresses a desire to be at the bedside as a family member dies, let him be there. Excluding a child who is interested and who wants to participate may somehow make him feel guilty or make him think that he is to blame for the death.

A child who has lost a loved one will be extremely sensitive about being separated from the adults he loves and trusts. If a parent needs to leave he should explain carefully to the child where he is going, what he will be doing, and what time he will return. Take the child with you if you can.

Likewise, if at all possible don't send the child away right after the death. First of all, it might unnecessarily panic the child; his father went away and isn't coming back, and now he's being sent away, too. Second, the child may feel he's being punished for the death. It's important for the child to feel part of the family unit and to have the support of the other members of his family at this time. It is much better if the child can stay at home, in familiar surroundings, where he can sleep in his own bed, play with his own toys, and sit in his own special chair at the dinner table.

Make special efforts to keep the child involved in preparing for the funeral and burial. Even the youngest child can help; a preschooler, for instance, could assist by answering the door as friends and associates come to offer sympathy. Older children could help by preparing light refreshments to serve those who come to visit; by writing thank-you notes to those who bring flowers, cards, or other gifts; or by housecleaning, cooking, or preparation of clothing to be worn to the funeral.

Above all, make sure that a child is told about the death immediately. A woman who had lost her husband was overcome with grief and confusion about how to approach her ten-year-old daughter; she delayed giving the child the news, and before she was able to do it as she had planned the girl found out about the death from a neighbor. The woman, in delaying what had to be done, lost a precious opportunity to share with her daughter an event that would affect her entire life.

Children, as well as adults, need to bid farewell to their loved ones. This can either be done at a funeral, a burial rite, or later at the cemetery. You should always provide the child with the opportunity of attending the funeral or burial rite; children who are excluded may worry needlessly about what is happening at the funeral and may even become concerned that more deaths will occur. But never force a child to attend a funeral; some will not want to go. Either way, explain carefully what the funeral is—tell the child that it is a special meeting held to honor the dead person, a time when friends and family members can express their love and appreciation for all the fine things the dead person accomplished during her lifetime. If the child does decide to attend try to sit in a place where you can answer his questions as the funeral proceeds without disturbing others. Don't leave a child alone at a funeral.

If the child decides not to attend give him the opportunity of accompanying you to the cemetery at some later time when he seems ready. Giving him the chance to put some flowers at the grave site will help him say good-bye to the dead person and will help him express love and appreciation.

Your feelings following the death should not be hidden from the child; children are extremely perceptive, and your child will be able to tell what you are feeling. Children who receive one message verbally and another message nonverbally become suspicious and mistrustful. You should be open and honest about your feelings; if you are sad tell your child that you are sad. Of course, there is an important exception to this rule: a child should be spared from "participating" in a complete emotional breakdown suffered by an adult he depends on for emotional security. If you or another adult in your household should suffer such a breakdown take care to keep the child unaware of the intensity of the situation. But do not remove the child from the home or the suffering adult from the home if at all possible; separation of this kind immediately following a death can cause the child to fear that another death has occurred.

As you grieve the loss of the loved one talk to your child. Explain that you are not grieving for the dead person—explain that the dead person is peaceful and free of pain—but that you are grieving for yourself because you have lost a relationship that was valuable to you. Let your child know that such grief is normal and that it will pass with time. Help your child to understand that we all have different feelings at a time like this and that we are sometimes confused and hurt; make your child feel that his own reaction is normal and healthy and that he will feel better as time passes.

Answer a child's questions honestly; it is important not to lie to a child. As a parent or someone close to a child you are the best judge of what the child is ready to handle; you might need to tell him only part of the truth until he is ready to handle more, but you should never deliberately lie to him.

Let your child know that he can always talk to you and that if he has any questions you will answer them. Then make sure that you answer the child in language and terminology that he can understand. For a two-year-old you might say, "Daddy is dead. He can no longer eat, or sleep, or run, or play."

Don't use phrases like "going to sleep," "resting," or "going away" to describe death to a child. A child who thinks that a father who is dead simply "went away" may become hysterical at the thought of his mother leaving him with a babysitter while she goes to a movie with some friends. After all, his father "went away" and never came back. A child who is told that someone who is dying is "going to sleep" may refuse to take a nap and may struggle to stay awake all night for fear of dying himself.

Share religious concepts with a child, but make sure that you do so in language he can understand: "Some grown-ups like to think that when people die, their bodies lie in special boxes in the cemetery, but their spirits—the part of them that we love—are in a special place called heaven, where there is no unhappiness and where there is no war or pain." If you do not believe in an afterlife, however, you should not present such a concept to a child just in the hopes of comforting him; children are quick to sense deceit and dishonesty. If they think that you are not being honest they will feel less secure and will experience more severe grief symptoms.

Don't deny a child's feelings. They are real to him. Some people, thinking that a child is "too young to understand," fail to acknowledge the turmoil a child may be experiencing. You need to recognize and face up to a child's feelings before you can expect him to recognize them.

Pay special attention to a child who develops symptoms of illness following the death of a loved one—such symptoms are usually emotionally induced and are not indicative of real physical disease, but they are painful and frightening to the child. This is especially true if the child lost a loved one to a painful, debilitating disease, such as cancer, the child will be extremely frightened of any pain in himself, either real or imagined. Reassure the child with something like, "I know that your tummy really hurts. I'll bet if you ate some ice cream, it would feel better. Your tummy ache will go away; it's not like the sickness that your daddy had. You will feel better soon."

In some cases a child may experience pathological grief and need professional help. A child who maintains an unshakable fixation on the lost person, who continues to believe for longer than a week that the dead person will return, who is not able to do schoolwork several months after the death, or who becomes severely hostile or delinquent probably needs professional help.

Remember that children are individuals, and each child will react differently to the death of a loved one. Some seem to be unfeeling and empty. Others adjust well. Some children deny the fact; others are angry or rebellious. There is no "normal" reaction among children because so much depends on the child's emotional development at the time of the death and on the child's preparation for the death. As a parent it is important that you understand your child and that you reassure him throughout the death experience.

In addition to the things you can do for your child you can prepare yourself as a parent while your child is still an infant by sorting out your own feelings. Decide exactly how you feel about death; come to terms with your own beliefs and opinions. If you are uncomfortable about the way you feel seek opportunities to talk with other adults about death and the dying experience. You will be much better able to help your child cope with death if you are secure about your feelings.

GRIEVING PARENTS

It is easier to come to terms with the death of a person who lived a full and happy life, who had a pleasing career, who married, who reared children, and who was able to experience all of the joys and sorrows life has to offer than it is to accept the death of a child who was not able to live to experience any of the things that life holds for most of us. For that reason it is extremely difficult for parents to adjust to the death of a child.

Other things also make the death of a child particularly difficult.[14] First of all, death is not as common now as it used to be. Infant and child mortality rates used to be quite high, and we were *practiced* with child death; now, however, modern technology and medical advances have significantly reduced that mortality rate, so we do not experience the death of children nearly as often.

Second, parents are in such a position of responsibility for children—for all of their physical needs as well as their spiritual and emotional ones—that they often feel somehow responsible for a child who dies. They feel that they in some way must have caused the death: they failed to feed the child properly, to bathe him enough, or to cuddle him often enough. This wrong assumption of responsibility leaves parents consumed with guilt and unable to progress through a normal grief experience.

Third, parents receive little social support after the death of a child. Support at such a time is critical; a number of things can be done to help parents and family after the death of a child.[15]

You should encourage the parents to talk openly and honestly with the physician that attended the child. The physician should be able to reassure them

[14]Thomas Helmrath and Elaine M. Steinitz, "Death of an Infant: Parental Grieving and the Failure of Social Support," *Journal of Family Practice*, 6, no. 4 (1978), 785.

[15]Compiled from Helmrath and Steinitz, "Death of an Infant"; Kathleen F. Gaffney, "Helping Grieving Parents," *JEN*, July/August 1976, pp. 42-43; Linda Murray, "The Dying Child's Family," *Practical Psychology for Physicians*, August 1976, pp. 58-62; Margaret S. Miles, "SIDS: Parents Are the Patients," *JEN*, March/April 1977, pp. 29-32; George J. Gilson, "Care of the Family Who Has Lost a Newborn," *Postgraduate Medicine*, 60, no. 6 (December 1976), 67-70.

that everything possible was done to help the child and that the parents were not responsible in any way for what happened to the child.

Both parents should be encouraged to express their grief openly. Father, especially, may think that it is not "manly" to break down and cry. It is important, though, for *both* parents to express fully the grief they are feeling. It is also important for them to express their sadness in front of the other children, who need to know that their own feelings of sadness are both normal and acceptable.

Acknowledge the parents' grief. One woman explained that she had a great deal of support throughout her pregnancy; one friend even called her every day to chat, see how she was feeling, and offer help with the other children or the grocery shopping. The baby died thirty hours after birth. The woman explained that after the baby's death no one even wanted to talk about the baby. People didn't mention it; she was expected to go on as if nothing happened. Parents who lose a child, even a newborn, need to talk about it and need to have others face the fact of death with them. Take your cues from the parents involved—if they want to talk about the baby or the experience of dying be a good listener.

Encourage the couple to communicate freely between themselves. Sometimes a wife may be confused and hurt because she doesn't think her husband is feeling the effects of the death as strongly as she is; the husband, on the other hand, may wrongly feel that he needs to stay strong so that his wife will have someone to lean on. Both should frankly and honestly confront their emotions and should share with each other the support of understanding.

Never react adversely to a parent who is expressing grief. Parents, like all who grieve, need to feel free to express their feelings without fear of being rejected for them.

If the couple thinks it would be comforting help arrange for them to talk to another couple who has undergone a similar experience—losing a child shortly after birth, or suffering through a terminal illness of a young child.

THE DEATH OF INFANTS

An especially difficult situation is that of the newborn or infant who dies. A woman who has eagerly anticipated the birth of her child—who has crocheted delicate booties and chosen a name and painted an old crib a cheery yellow —faces a unique anguish if her child is born dead or dies within days of its birth. Her situation is made worse by the fact that in most hospitals staffs are ill-equipped to deal with her and so she is treated like every other mother in the masternity ward.[16] This lack of support has resulted in severe psychiatric disorders among women who have suffered the loss of a newborn.

[16] John H. Kennell, "Helping Parents Cope with Perinatal Death," *Contemporary OB/GYN,* July 1978, pp. 53-68.

A common misconception that we only mourn the deaths of people with whom we have established an intimate and long-standing relationship fosters misunderstandings that can lead to cruel and senseless remarks. A twenty-two-year-old mother whose child was stillborn reported that friends who came to see her after her release from the hospital made statements such as, "You can always have another baby," "At least you never knew him or really got attached," or "The baby is probably better off dead, anyway, because he was probably damaged." Amazingly, a number of the visitors avoided the subject entirely and acted as though nothing had happened.

A mother does not have to cradle an infant in her arms to initiate feelings of attachment; most women report such feelings soon after fetal movement is first felt, and the feelings of attachment grow stronger during the months the child is carried in the womb. Many women have dreams about the infant—what the child will be like, what kind of a mother she will be, what kind of a personality the baby will have. To many the baby is a firm reality long before it is born. And, of course, the mourning becomes even more intense if the child lives for a short time and has been fondled, nurtured, and cared for by its mother.

Some reactions are normal among women who lose newborns that are usually not manifest among those in other grief situations. Most are overcome by tormenting guilt. Because the baby's health and welfare is so closely attached to the mother through the placenta most women blame themselves for smoking too much, eating improperly, or even experiencing stressful emotions. They blame themselves for gaining too much weight or not gaining enough weight, for taking aspirin for a cold, for drinking a martini. It is important for such a woman to express her fears and doubts to her doctor, so that the doctor can reassure her that she had no control over what happened.

Another unique grief reaction among mothers is the effect of the death on the woman's other relationships, especially the one with her husband, because of her tendency to respond to others with anger and irritability, feelings that surface as she blames herself for her child's death. Still another effect of the grief is the remarkable change manifest in daily routines; women are unable to organize household chores, make simple decisions, or complete projects. Some only perform household duties if they are pushed into them by a husband or demanding child.

What can you do to help a woman in such a situation? First, and foremost, allow her to ventilate her feelings. She probably needs to cry; she should be allowed to do so, and should not be given a tranquilizer unless her grief becomes abnormal and interferes with her own health. Let her talk about the loss; acknowledge it as a real loss, and let her know that you understand how she feels. Listen to her.

It is important that you help establish the literal existence of the baby—something that is hard to do if the baby never lived outside the mother's body. Ask hospital staff members if the mother can touch the baby and examine it closely; some hospitals allow mothers to clean and diaper their babies after they are dead. If the mother was unconscious at the time of birth arrange for her to go to the mortuary, where she can look at the baby closely, and perhaps hold it, in private surroundings.

If the mother is still in the hospital when the baby is prepared for burial, arrange to take a picture of the baby, even though it is dead, so that the mother can see the child. It is a good idea to let the mother see the baby, or a picture of the baby, even if it is deformed; this gives the physician or some other person the opportunity to point out the baby's perfections in addition to its problems. Most mothers imagine deformities much worse than those that actually exist; many may be put at ease if they are allowed to see the baby or its picture.

If the parents want to do so encourage them to give a stillborn baby a name; this helps establish the reality of the child and helps parents later when they want to talk about the baby. A final way of establishing the baby's reality is to have a funeral for the child. Besides formalizing the baby's death as an event worthy of time and attention, the funeral service allows friends and family members to congregate and offer support and concern for the parents. Many parents derive religious comfort from a funeral service or burial rite.

SUDDEN INFANT DEATH SYNDROME

The death of an infant who succumbs to Sudden Infant Death Syndrome (SIDS), a mysterious killer that claims infants for no apparent reason any time after the first week of life, is especially disturbing.[17] Lack of knowledge concerning SIDS and misinformation often cause unnecessary grief and anguish for parents, who blame themselves for the infant's death.

SIDS families are different from other families in which children die. Losing a child who has a congenital heart condition or leukemia or some other disease that has given the parents warning is very different from finding a perfectly normal-seeming baby dead in the crib. It is even different from an accidental death; if a child dies in an automobile accident or falls down the stairs, you can see the cause and effect. But an SIDS death is not only sudden—it seems completely unreasonable. There are two losses for the parents: loss of a loved one and loss of a part of the self.[18]

It's important to learn the facts surrounding SIDS so you can help correct misinformation. SIDS cannot be predicted or prevented, even by a doctor; its cause is unknown. Babies do not suffocate, choke, or breathe in vomited materi-

---

[17] "Facts about Sudden Infant Death Syndrome" (Chicago: National Sudden Infant Death Syndrome Foundation, 1978).

[18] Stanley E. Weinstein, *Mental Health Issues in Grief Counseling* (Baltimore, Md.: U.S. Department of Health, Education, and Welfare, 1979), DHEW Publication Number (HSA) 79-5264, n.p.

al, even though these are sometimes wrongly listed on death certificates. Most babies are entirely healthy before death; they do not suffer.

SIDS is not a contagious disease; other babies and children cannot "catch" it. It rarely occurs in children over seven months of age, and it is not hereditary. It is no more likely to occur in one family than in another.

Commonly called crib death, SIDS has completely baffled the medical profession for years. There is usually no sign of a struggle; autopsies reveal no apparent physical cause of death. Some children may be twisted in their bedding, leading parents or emergency medical technicians to decide wrongly that the baby died of suffocation. Even in cases where a baby was lying face down and was covered with blankets, sufficient oxygen was available to prevent suffocation. Most SIDS victims have a bloody froth around the mouth or nose when discovered by parents, but this froth appears *after* death and is not an indication that the baby vomited and choked.

Because crib death is impossible to prevent or predict *no one is responsible* when a baby dies from SIDS. Yet the guilt and torment suffered by parents or babysitters make them the real victims.

One way to help parents is to make them understand that no one, most particularly the parents, is at fault. SIDS is not a result of medication given to the child, is not hereditary, and is not a result of breastfeeding or too many blankets in the crib. You might consider obtaining some information on SIDS if the parents' doctor has not already given them some. Detailed brochures about SIDS have been written especially for parents.

Another comforting thought for the parents is that the baby did not suffer pain; many parents suffer incredible anguish thinking of a helpless infant enduring pain violent enough to cause death. Some babies appear to be in pain when they are discovered—their faces look like they are distorted with pain. This distortion, though, is usually caused by the normal muscle contraction that accompanies death, rigor mortis. Babies who die of SIDS do not cry out as they are dying—as they would certainly do if they were suffering pain—but instead die silently. In many cases babies have died during a nap when a parent or babysitter was in the next room and would have readily heard even the slightest stirring. Death from SIDS is generally rapid, rarely lasting longer than five minutes. In many cases death is instant.

Encourage the parents to talk. Resist the urge to ignore the topic because it makes you uncomfortable. Offer your sympathy, and face the situation squarely. Help the parents express their own feelings, even if those feelings are embarrassing to you or even if they are feelings of rage and hostility. Listen to what they have to say—they need someone to talk to. If they will let you help the parents in some physical, tangible way. Offer to make phone calls if there are relatives that need to be informed; bring them a meal.

The grief reaction of fathers may differ radically from the grief reaction of mothers following an SIDS death. Women more often express the desire to talk about the death; men more often avoid talking about the experience. A probable contributing factor is a product of life-style: a man is often able to divert himself by going to work and concentrating on his colleagues or the demands of his job; if the woman does not work outside the home she is forced to stay at home and care for other children, an environment rich with constant reminders of the dead baby, the death experience, and the ongoing mourning.

Special care needs to be taken if there are other children in the home who are old enough to comprehend what has happened to the baby. One, or preferably both, of the parents should sit down with the other children in the family and should explain carefully and precisely what happened. Children who are old enough to understand should be given all the facts of SIDS; all children should be told that the baby died from a *disease*. All children should also be told that the disease that killed the baby strikes only a few babies of *that* age, and each child should be reassured that the disease was *not* contagious and that there is no danger of other children in the family "catching" the disease or dying from the same disease.

LOSING A SPOUSE

Losing a spouse, whether through death or divorce, is one of the severest kinds of losses experienced by modern men and women. Most of us are dependent on our partners for physical fulfillment, emotional needs, and all kinds of complex supports. When those supports are suddenly withdrawn the adjustment may take a great deal of active work on the part of the widow or widower, or divorced partner, and may require help from others outside the family. Even though the mate is gone, the emotional feeling for him or her is still very much alive. It is very much like the pain an amputee often feels in the dismembered limb.

You can help to soften the blow of losing your spouse in several ways.[19]

1. Set some immediate goals, even if they are simple ones, to give yourself a sense of accomplishment. You are lacking the familiar support of another person, so it is important that you stay busy and feel a sense of accomplishment and usefulness.

2. If possible enroll for a class at a nearby university or college. You may be able to center your mind temporarily on things other than the loss of your spouse by involving yourself in a challenging, stimulating learning experience.

3. Many who lose a spouse, suffer real financial setbacks, either through medical bills or the loss of income. Seek help and advice in managing a financial crisis.

[19] Adapted with permission from Jane Gunther, "How To Survive Widowhood," *Reader's Digest* (June 1975), 181-86.

4. Avoid isolation; loneliness is one of the greatest problems that follows losing a spouse. Hold on to the friends that you and your spouse shared; they will still like you even if your spouse is not here anymore. You will probably feel more comfortable interacting on a one-to-one basis with another couple or hosting a party where both single people and couples are invited. It will help to avoid strictly "couple" situations. Don't feel stupid about going to parties or other social activities without a partner; the host likes *you*, or you wouldn't have been invited. Or try going out with members of your own sex; there's nothing wrong with enjoying dinner at a restaurant with a group of women or men you've always liked and admired. Daily contact with others helps keep your mind occupied and gives you something meaningful to concentrate on and new problems to solve.

5. Don't make too many sudden changes in your life-style following the loss of a spouse. You need time to adjust to the shock of being alone, and it is helpful to be in familiar surroundings. Your thoughts are not clearly rational at a time like this, and you may make decisions in haste that you will regret later.

6. Listen to the advice of others, but don't be pressured into something you are uncomfortable about just because well-meaning friends or relatives are pressuring you. Make your own decisions; you need to be in control of your own life.

7. Do not be afraid to ask for help. There are agencies, physicians, and psychologists who specialize in helping those who have lost spouses; you shouldn't feel embarrassed about asking for help or asking for support to help you through a difficult period.

Grief and mourning will affect all of us and will become a part of all our lives at some time or another. How much easier it will be to cope with loss when we understand the processes of mourning, when we are able to understand that our feelings are normal and acceptable, and when we know enough to recognize when those feelings are *not* normal, and are sensible enough to seek help.

Grief and mourning will run their course, and they will leave us all the wiser and better equipped to meet whatever consequences may face us down the road.

EUTHANASIA

During her pregnancy with her first child Suzanne had experienced a great deal of difficulty falling asleep, and when it did come her sleep was restless and shallow. As a result her general health level declined; she lacked energy and was susceptible to colds and other minor infections. Then she discovered thalidomide, a tranquilizer marketed in Germany; it was a drug that offered a good night's sleep, left no hangover, was not habit-forming, and, incredibly, overdoses could not kill. In fact it was considered so safe that it was sold without a prescription, and women throughout the world relied on it to help them through the difficult first months of pregnancy. Suzanne was among those women.

At the end of her pregnancy Suzanne's daughter was born, a victim of horrible deformity. The baby had no arms or legs, her face was completely disfigured, and her anal canal emptied into her vagina.

Suzanne was consumed with grief and obtained a prescription for a strong barbituate from her physician. She took the drugs home, administered them to her baby, and ended the child's suffering.

- Gary and Pam had wanted a child ever since they had married seven years earlier and were thrilled beyond belief when Pam learned that she was pregnant one spring. They busied themselves with preparations for the baby. Pam learned to crochet, and she fashioned booties and sweaters and hats. Gary, handy with a hammer, converted the extra bedroom into a nursery, complete with ruffled curtains and built-in shelves for powder, lotion, and diaper pins. They bought a used crib and splashed it with sunny yellow paint.

Their eager anticipations were destroyed one snowy December morning when their son was born a victim of Down's syndrome, mongoloid idiocy. He rested in Pam's arms, a picture of concomitant oblique eyes, clubbed fingers, set-back ears, eye folds, and fat scruff on his neck. Pam and Gary knew that he would live a short life and that even the time he did live would be characterized by heart trouble, respiratory and digestive ailments, and arrested mental development.

Several hours after birth the baby did develop respiratory problems. Pam and Gary conferred with the physician, and the baby was placed in a sanitarium without any respiratory devices. Two days later, he died.[1]

- As the leaves turned colors one sultry autumn, Maria, a vital eighty-year-old who had immigrated to America from Italy, began to get sick. As the weather took on the familiar chill of winter her ailments increased. She became weak and pale; one morning while going out for the mail she slipped on the ice and fractured her hip. She was hospitalized, and the full impact of her predicament became obvious. In addition to her fractured hip she was suffering with pneumonia and a myriad of painful infections that sapped her strength. Her days became a legend of pain and discomfort.

Shortly before Christmas hospital aides who were making their rounds were standing by Maria's bed when her pulse suddenly started to drop. While they stood around in frenzied confusion about what to do Maria's doctor rushed into the room and—contrary to his own orders—actively worked on resuscitation. Maria's pulse got a little stronger; the crisis had passed.

Three days later, on Christmas Eve, Maria's condition had become pitiful. She lay in the bed, a pale, yellowed figure, hunched up with pain, struggling for every breath. Her doctor entered her room quietly and stood, looking at her in her shameful condition. After a few minutes of agonizing thought he stopped the resuscitator and pulled out the intravenous tubes that had given her nourishment for so many weeks. The next morning Maria was dead.[2]

- At age seventeen, John was the president of his high school student body and was active in debate, football, and the school's concert band. During the last

---

[1] Adapted from Bernard Bard and Joseph Fletcher, "The Right to Die," *Atlantic Monthly*, April 1968, pp. 59-64. ©by Bernard Bard.

[2] Adapted from "Why Prolong Life?" *National Observer*, March 4, 1972, p. 1.

several months he had received recognition for his outstanding academic achievements, and, in every right, he was looking forward to a long, active, energetic life.

The afternoon was unusually crisp for October, and the clouds of steam escaped with every breath as the group of uniform-clad gridders pressed close in a huddle. It was a risky play, but they were going to try it. John would swing wide and pass the ball to Nathan, who would carry it through the end zone.

The ball was snapped into his eager hands, and John started the run to the edge of the field. Suddenly a tearing pain ripped through his body; hit from behind with unusual force, he catapulted forward and landed hard in a grotesquely twisted position. His helmet cracked; his neck was broken.

Paramedics ran onto the field; the coach was afraid John had stopped breathing. Hours later in the brightly lit emergency room the terrible truth became known: John had stopped breathing and his heart had stopped beating for almost ten minutes—long enough to cause severe destruction of brain tissue. John might survive, the doctor muttered grimly, but he'd be a vegetable. He could never think, speak, walk, or carry a football again. He'd never stand at a debate podium or play the trombone. He was in a coma, and he lay perfectly still on the sterile bed. A machine breathed for him; another machine helped keep his heart beating. Two tubes ran to his stomach—one through each nostril—and food was passed into his digestive tract. Other tubes, run into the veins in his arms, provided him with nourishment and essential medication. The doctor stepped into the hallway and talked with John's parents; maybe he should disconnect the machines and let John die with some dignity.

John's father reacted with horror. He had not given up hope. He knew how much his son loved life and didn't think he had the right to pass a death sentence on a boy who had been so vital. So they waited.

Surprisingly, John gained weight. He remained in a coma for months; each day at 5:30 his father came to visit him. He'd sit on the edge of John's bed and discuss all kinds of things with him. Nurses who moved in and out of the tomblike room heard John's father telling him about his brother's Boy Scout hike, his mother's fledgling attempt at skiing, the family's new pet. Most of the hospital personnel belived that John could not hear or think; his father, though, thought there might be a dim chance that his son could hear, and he couldn't bear the thought of the loneliness he must have felt during the long days and nights.

One day it happened—John fluttered into consciousness. His conscious condition passed as quickly and unexpectedly as it had come, but he continued to move in and out of the daylight until, one evening, he came out of his coma completely.

It was a long, difficult, uphill struggle for John, but he overcame tremendous odds and underwent a rigorous physical therapy program. He began speaking again; one morning the doctor came into the room to discover John standing at a window, looking out at the summer sun; John had walked to the window unassisted. And, because of his father's faith and refusal to abandon hope, John had every reason to expect a happy and fulfilling future.

• Anne and Ray had eagerly anticipated the time when their children would marry and start their own families so that they could spend time together doing all of the things that rearing a family had not left them the time or the resources to do before. They were discouraged when Anne was diagnosed as having multiple sclerosis shortly before their youngest daughter entered college.

Anne's days became a series of pain-filled obstacles; her movements were stiff and jerky, and parts of her body were numb, devoid of any feeling at all. Ray took over many of the chores Anne had always done.

One April day Ray complained of flulike symptoms; Anne insisted that he see a doctor, and nothing appeared to be wrong. Two months later, while at work, Ray collapsed and blacked out.

The diagnosis? Probable tumor of the brain. Ray was wheeled into surgery, where the prognosis was grim; the tumor was so massive that to remove it surgically would leave Ray completely incapacitated, a virtual vegetable. The tables had been turned—Anne had always expected to die first, but now she was told that her husband didn't have long to live.

Anne and Ray lived the next year to the fullest. They walked hand-in-hand through meadows and parks and enjoyed picnics with the children. They went on a thirteen-day Caribbean cruise, something they had always dreamed about. And then the treatments began taking their toll.

Ray's auburn hair was burned off by the cobalt treatments, and he started losing his memory. The cobalt treatments were extremely unpleasant; Ray would vomit and then pass out. He lost his ability to think clearly; he became emaciated and weak.

When Ray entered the hospital for the last time he weighed eighty pounds less than he had when the tumor had been diagnosed. He was blind, and his pain was excruciating. Anne knew that there was much that could be done to prolong her husband's life—oxygen tents, intravenous feedings, resuscitators—but she couldn't bear the thought of his constant pain, of his lying in a hospital, covered with bandages and with tubes thrust into every opening. Her orders to Ray's doctors were strict: do everything possible to keep him out of pain, but do nothing except keep him comfortable. No medical hocus-pocus.

A few days later Ray was dead; Anne was relieved. He was out of pain. A neighbor expressed surprise at Anne's decision to terminate medical help for Ray, but Anne was firm: "I hope that when I get too bad, somebody will love me enough, the way I loved Ray, to do the same for me."

• Don, a sixty-eight-year-old doctor, was admitted to the hospital with advanced cancer of the stomach; when physicians operated on him they discovered that the cancer had affected his liver, too. A second operation was performed to remove Don's stomach, and that operation showed signs that the cancer had spread further still.

The surgeons conferred with Don, and as a result of his extensive medical career he understood fully his condition. Despite constant administrations of powerful drugs Don's pain was unceasing and agonizing. Ten days after the operation to remove his stomach he collapsed because of a clot in his lung; another operation was required to save his life.

As he struggled in the recovery process Don drew his surgeon aside. Expressing appreciation for his efforts and faith in his skill, Don asked nevertheless that, should he have another collapse, he be allowed to die peacefully; the pain was too intense, and he was unable to bear it much longer. He wrote a note to that effect and had the surgeon place it in his case files, and he discussed the matter personally with hospital staff members who were part of his treatment team. He took great effort to make sure everyone understood his feelings.

Two weeks later he had a heart attack; contrary to his wishes he was resuscitated. The same night his heart stopped again *four times;* each time the hospital team scrambled to revive him.

Don lingered on for three more weeks; his intense suffering was marked by violent vomiting and convulsions. Blood transfusions, intravenous feeding, and involved drug therapy, kept him alive; his heart had stopped, so many times that his brain cells were dying from oxygen starvation. Finally his heart stopped again, and hospital technicians were not able to revive it, despite every effort.[3] Obviously, the question of the right to die is a complex and highly volatile one. Proponents of the right to die—dying with dignity or euthanasia, both passive and active—tell us that death is often less cruel than a life filled with pain and misery, that death to a suffering person is a blessing and a relief. They believe that every person has the right to die a dignified death, not a death marked by excruciating pain and mindless vegetation. Opponents warn us sternly that none of us has the right to play God, that the right to give life and the right to take away life rests with a higher power than the human family. They believe that we are bound by duty and honor to do everything possible to sustain life. In answer, proponents tell us that "life" is not valuable or real if it is simply a battered existence of pain and agony and tubes and resuscitators. Opponents answer back that "life" is life if the heart is beating and the lungs are expanding with air—no matter what the condition of the mind.

Is there a difference between failing to start life-saving treatment and stopping life-saving treatment once it has been initiated? Is there a moral and ethical difference between "letting" someone die by withholding treatment and "killing" someone by offering a painless termination of life?

Statements released by the American Medical Association are purposefully

---

[3] Adapted from Neil Elliott, *The Gods of Life* (New York/London: Macmillan Publishing Co., Inc., 1074), pp. 85-86. Copyright © 1974 by Neil Elliott.

vague, but one sentiment rings through with stunning clarity: the doctor must never kill a patient. So far there hasn't been a ruling about "letting" a patient die as a result of neglecting to offer treatment, only the definite ruling that a doctor should never *kill* a patient by giving a deadly dose of medicine, disconnecting life-saving machinery, or giving a patient opportunity and instruction for killing himself.[4]

Exactly what makes the issue so difficult for physicians to deal with? There are ten major areas of ethical uncertainty connected with the entire issue of euthanasia, or "mercy killing":[5]

1. *Death usually isn't instantaneous.*   There are several stages of death: clinical death, in which the heart stops beating and the person stops breathing; brain death, in which brain activity ceases and brain cells die from lack of oxygen; and cellular death, in which the cells of various body organs die. These organs die at different rates, and even when part of an organ has died the entire organ has not undergone total destruction. So when is a person *dead*? His heart may have stopped beating, but his brain may still be active and his other organs alive. On the other hand, a person may be breathing and experiencing a heart-beat maintained by a machine, but his brain may have ceased all activity. His blood is still circulating, so is he alive, or is he dead because he cannot think? Can a physician pull the plug on a patient whose brain has stopped functioning, even though blood is circulating? Or can he stop trying to resuscitate someone whose heart has stopped beating, even though his brain is very much alive?

2. *There is no solid definition of professional etiquette and professional ethics.*   Professional etiquette and ethics demand that a physician exercise courtesy and concern for his patients and that he exercise courtesy and concern for his colleagues. What happens when his concern for a patient clouds his ability to judge a course of action? Or what happens when, as in Don's case, the patient is another doctor, and he demands to be left alone? Where does respect enter in here?

3. *The physician's own interests and idealism inevitably enter the picture.* Often the doctor's interests and his idealism come into conflict, such as when an elderly patient who has no ability to pay for expensive long-term medical treatment requires it to be kept alive. Should a doctor burden the patient and his family and possibly not receive pay, or should the doctor allow the elderly person to die?

4. *Medical truth is not absolute.*   There is the truth as it relates to the

---

[4]Karen Waugh Zucker, "Legislatures Provide for Death with Dignity," *Journal of Legal Medicine,* August 1977, pp. 21-23.

[5]"Mercy Killing," *Encyclopedia of Health Sciences* (Stanford, Calif.: Medical Readings Incorporated, 1974), 13:1263.

patient and the truth as seen through the eyes of the physician. So many things affect the "truth"; every patient poses a unique, individual case in which the truth may be entirely different than that which applies to a patient a week later in a different hospital. For a stable, alert patient a detailed and complete diagnosis might constitute the "truth"; for a patient who might not be able to accept news of his impending death, a partial report of his condition may be the "truth."

5. *Medical mores change and respond to cultural changes.* A good example of changing medical and cultural mores is abortion—a medical practice that was unheard of in this country even fifty years ago except in the most extreme cases and that is now legal in several states and is performed in many others as a result of intense pressure by women's groups. But cultural pressures are an inadequate reason for any medical more to be changed. And before such changes can be recognized widely in the medical community legislation and/or judicial action needs to be enacted to define exact boundaries.

6. *Man has two dimensions: He is creative, and he is a creature.* Doctors who spend years studying and practicing medicine can use their creativity in devising new methods of treatment and new ways to prolong life. No matter what they do, however, and no matter how long they succeed in postponing it, nature eventually rules supreme and exercises her power of death. So, in that aspect, each human being is only a creature, subject to the whims of nature.

7. *The welfare of the many sometimes conflicts with the welfare of the few.* Of course, a physician's primary concern is with the individual who lies at his mercy as a patient. But he must of necessity also be concerned with that patient's family. It may seem kind to shorten the life of a terminally ill patient who is suffering with pain or weakness, but his family may have very valid reasons for wanting him kept alive. The family has the responsibility for final disposition of the patient's body after death finally works its course, so they must be able to exercise an opinion about the patient's final stages of medical care. On the other hand, a patient who is terminally ill may be placing a severe financial drain on a family, a hardship from which they may never recover, if he is allowed to vegetate day after day in a hospital bed—costing family members an estimated $50,000 a year.

8. *Physicians are expected to regulate themselves.* Physicians are expected every day to make moral decisions—some minor, such as *how* to treat a patient, and some major, such as whether to allow a patient to die. They are generally protected from prosecution and are generally free from restricting supervision. This freedom is cherished by most physicians, and yet it becomes a difficult burden when the physician is confronted with a painful, confusing situation concerning the life and death of an individual patient.

9. *Technology has perhaps advanced beyond wisdom.*   New technology is being developed at such a rapid pace that it is difficult, sometimes impossible, for physicians to keep up a current and workable understanding of how to put that new technology to use in their individual practices. And there is an even deeper complication when it comes to the terminally ill; many of the terminally ill are elderly, and many more are so weakened and devastated by their conditions that it is almost impossible for the physician to judge how they will react to a treatment involving new technology. Further, some physicians are resistant to change and are reluctant to begin using new technology that may needlessly prolong a patient's life.

10. *Problems arise from the concept of a "useful" life.*   Is it worth prolonging a life that is no longer "useful," that only becomes a scenario of pain-wracked hospital residence? Is it worth prolonging the life of an individual who has become a mindless vegetable, a man or woman who can only lie in a bed, fed through tubes and breathing through a machine, who will never think or run or talk again? What, exactly, is "life"?

All of these are difficult questions and dilemmas, and many of them do not have answers. For some of them, though, we can consider these guidelines.[6]

1. The definition of a human being ultimately has to do with that human being's ability to communicate. Communication of thoughts and logical ideas is what separates man from all the species of animals and vegetables on the earth; it is what makes him unique. The prolonging of life in a human being who has permanently lost the ability to communicate should be seriously questioned.

2. Producing pain or suffering without purpose in an innocent human being should be considered criminal. Experimental techniques that may cause such pain and suffering and that may not be of real benefit should be seriously questioned, especially when dealing with the elderly, the very young, and the unknowing.

3. Because the physician is a professional he is entitled to the privilege of consulting colleagues and gaining the best in their advice and the result of their experience. But there are times when a physician is solely responsible for a patient's welfare, and during those times a decision cannot be abrogated by him; he must be willing to be decisive at such a time and to live by the decision he makes.

4. There are three different kinds of euthanasia: (a) the withdrawal of drugs that may serve to prolong life artificially; (b) the administration of pain-relieving

[6] George W. Paulson, "Who Should Live?" *Geriatrics,* March 1973, pp. 133-36.

drugs that may have the effect of accelerating the dying process; and (c) the administration of death-inducing agents. Many physicians apparently condone the first two practices, but few are willing to practice overt euthanasia—the administration of death-inducing agents.

5. Legislation may not be the real answer in some cases, because legislation only serves to introduce rigidity and to limit the physician's flexibility. Since each patient represents an individual case and an individual set of problems and considerations legislation may be more harmful than helpful. There is something that protects the individual much better than legislation: the concept of the physician-friend, or family practitioner. After all, killing impersonally and from a distance is much easier than killing a friend in a one-to-one human relationship.

6. If death seems to be the best answer to a patient's condition then the family should always be included in any discussion that may lead to that finality. The physician should honestly face the family and should explain to family members that death is not always unwelcome and frightening to a patient but is instead considered a blessing and a welcome relief.

We can perhaps further understand the issue of euthanasia or the right to die and better come to terms with all of its aspects if we examine the arguments presented by those who favor euthanasia and compare them with the arguments of those who are opposed to it.

ARGUMENTS FOR EUTHANASIA

George Washington, the first president of our country, after repeated bleedings, purgings, and blisterings (common medical practices of his time) begged his physicians, "I pray you take no more trouble for me. Let me go quietly." [7]

Some proponents of euthanasia agree that a patient should be given elementary, ordinary care, such as feeding and other regular nursing procedures, but they object to the use of "extraordinary support" for the terminally ill. Extraordinary support is usually defined as: [8]

- Artificial respirators used to promote breathing.
- Stimulation of the heart muscle by heart massage, pacemakers, or other machinery.
- Replacement or aid of worn-out kidneys by machinery.
- Transplantation of vital organs.

[7] Ibid., p. 136.
[8] Elliott, *The Gods of Life,* p. 83.

- Prolonged medication that acts to sustain or stabilize life or bodily functions (such as prolonged medication that stabilizes blood pressure).
- Prolonged intravenous feeding that replaces the natural intake and digestion of food.

Proponents of euthanasia seriously question the kindness or appropriateness of keeping alive a person whose only claim to life is that his body creates wastes and his blood is circulating. Notable among these patients are those with brain damage, with motor damage, or with pain so intense that it destroys the ability to think or concentrate on anything other than the pain. Through modern technology it is usually possible to keep people who are in a deep coma "alive" for months, even years, as has been done with Karen Anne Quinlan. Proponents of euthanasia, however, ask a significant question: is that patient really "alive"?

Those who favor euthanasia feel that human needs should be considered over and above human rights. Thus, they maintain that the person is of more value than merely being "alive" in the sense that the heart is beating and blood is circulating. These proponents claim that simply experiencing something—in this case, simply maintaining "life" by promoting circulation of blood and respiration—is not proof that this "life" is of worth or value to the individual himself.

This line of logic leads to the case for quality of life. Many feel that quality of life does not mean mere happiness while living, but it also includes all the conditions necessary for happiness. This means that in assessing quality of life we must realize that it is an entirely individual matter. It could be said that there is a quality of life for each individual—a quality that is considered livable for him—and when this quality is not realized, life can, by rights, be ended. The decision must be made for the benefit of the patient and no one else, taking into account a comparison of the conditions necessary for a quality life that the patient considers normal, desirable, and essential with those qualities of life that the patient actually possesses at that point in time. Do not make the mistake of interpreting this to mean that proponents of quality of life and its relation to euthanasia feel that this means that different people are of different values. On the contrary, they feel that all people are of equal value regardless of their physical or mental conditions. But they hasten to explain that not all lives are of equal value in a strictly biological sense. The value of a life depends upon the individual himself and his definition of value and quality.

When and if the decision is made to cease or not to initiate life-saving or life-support treatment, there is a continuing obligation to provide care and comfort for the patient, also taking into account care and support for the family members. "Neither physician nor patient are usually faced with only two options—to continue or discontinue life support treatment. The third option and continuing responsibility of health care professionals and families, no matter how damaged the patient's condition is to seek to improve the level of care and comfort of the dying, including being physically present to them."[9] This would include the limited use of apparatus but the use of extensive personal care and a therapeutic physical and social environment.

We are now able to cushion the uncomfortable effects of symptoms and prolong the lives of people with diseases that used to take life rapidly. Thus, it is felt that modern technology and treatment may indeed prolong life but in the process cause two unwanted effects: production of excruciating, intractable, or prolonged pain or suffering; and maintenance of a minimal capacity to experience and to relate with other human beings. Those who favor euthanasia use this as a strong defense. Nature obviously intended these diseases to work their course rapidly; left to her own devices nature will do the same today.

Other proponents stress the right of each individual to die with dignity. Many claim that the right to die is a basic constitutional right. They remind us of the sanctity of life, of the importance of a vital personality, of the torments suffered by those who are kept alive against their will. Is it, in essence, dignified to die "while comatose, betubed, aerated, glucosed, narcosed, sedated, not conscious, not even human anymore"?[10] These euthanasia proponents feel that a patient has a right to die his own, dignified death from causes that it is no longer merciful or reasonable to fight by medical intervention.

Many proponents of euthanasia even find some foundation for their beliefs in religion. They feel that God has deputized to man some of his dominion, so that man indeed has some control over his life. Therefore, we, as human beings, have much of the responsibility for our actions and decision making. However, even though those in favor of euthanasia have extrapolated some of their beliefs from religion, very few of them would be so bold as to contend that God is an actual advocate of euthanasia. They are merely saying that God gives us the power to make decisions; He doesn't necessarily condone the decisions made.

A strong argument can be made for euthanasia by appealing to our sensitivities, our compassion. Who among us would choose to have a sister, a husband, a mother, or a child suffer blinding pain with the ravages of a terminal illness? Who among us would not, in such a situation, much prefer the kinder alternative—death—and the blessing of peace for our loved ones?

In essence, proponents of euthanasia believe that there are two kinds of life: biological life, which consists of the vital and metabolic processes that promote and sustain the life of the body and the mind; and personal life, which includes experience; communication; personal responsibility for actions; social worth, utility, and status. "A great deal of experience and even some empirical data suggest that it is not so much (biological) life in itself which we desire, but

[9] Ibid., p. 96.

[10] Edward W. Keyserlingk, *Sanctity of Life or Quality of Life in the Context of Ethics, Medicine, and Law* (Ottawa, Canada: Law Reform Commission of Canada, 1979), p. 58.

bearable, enjoyable, and worthwhile experiences and satisfactions (personal life). We want life for what can be done with it, not for what it is in itself. 'It always seems to be assumed that life, of whatever quality, is the most priceless of possessions. Physicians often assume that patients would always prefer life, no matter how handicapped, to death. The opposite is often the case.' "[11]

Perhaps because euthanasia supporters do appeal to all of our higher emotions their viewpoint is easier to understand at times on an emotional level. It is then important to understand the arguments of the euthanasia critics, to hear their side of the story.

ARGUMENTS AGAINST EUTHANASIA

Here again it is important to remember that there are different levels of what we have called *euthanasia*. They range from simply withholding treatment, to stopping treatment that has already been undertaken, to actively causing death, for example, by administering lethal amounts of pain medication. Opponents to euthanasia are usually opposed to all of these degrees—opposed to any decision about regulating life and death.

Chief among the arguments used by critics of euthanasia is the belief that no human being has the right, under any circumstance, to decide that it is time for another human being to die.[12] Who, they ask, should ever place himself in the position of determining that another's life is no longer worth living?

While many patients obviously beg to be left alone and to be allowed to die, many more, these critics suggest, keep the door open to hope and faith in a continued existence. They struggle on, wanting for reasons only they can know to stay alive; to be helped to survive as long as possible. The practice of euthanasia, then, becomes only an excuse to say that we are qualified to decide that someone else's life is so low grade that it has ceased to be valuable either to himself or to others.

Another argument, and one that is important, is the one concerning motive. Euthanasia may be prompted by a motive other than compassion for the suffering patient; it may be the result of a financial decision to terminate life because of soaring costs of medical care, for instance. And other, more insidious, motives may enter in on the part of the physician and other members of the hospital staff, so that patients are actually killed for many reasons other than to gain a cessation of personal suffering. History has shown us too many tragic examples of men who were entrusted with too absolute a power.

Another argument counters the claim that a person who can no longer

[11] Keyserlingk, *Sanctity of Life*, p. 65.

[12] J.S. Habgood, "Euthanasia—A Christian View," *Royal Society of HCTH Journal,* 1979, 93:95.

communicate is less than human. The fact that the patient cannot communicate is significant. Because he cannot communicate he cannot tell us what joys are left in life for him; he cannot tell us what kind of personal life is still present for him; he cannot tell us what kind of future he anticipates; indeed, he cannot even tell us that he wants to live or die.[13]

Some argue that the concept of a living will is a good one, that we should be able legally to inform our family members, our physician, and our attorney that should we ever require artificial sustaining of life we would rather die. Some states have granted citizens the right to that decision. But who among us has not at some time in his life changed his mind, altered his opinion about some important philosophy or belief? We all have the right to change our minds, and, once we are in a position of facing death, we may view the situation from an entirely different prospect. And then it may be too late to change our minds. We may not be capable of expressing the fact that a change has indeed taken place.

And what of personal judgment? What of the failings that we are all subject to? What about making death the commonplace, making our power to decide life and death as cheap and ordinary as our power to decide which movie we will go to this weekend. As one doctor put it, "We shall start by putting patients away because they are in intolerable pain and haven't long to live anyway; and we shall end up by putting them away because it's Friday night and we want to get away for the weekend."[14] So, regardless of the original reasons for ending life, euthanasia can lead to wrongs of increasing magnitude such as this.

Among the medical profession the stiffest critics have relied on the argument that professionally they are unable to justify euthanasia—that they spoke the Hippocratic oath, promising to do everything in their power to sustain and save lives. Not just sometimes, or when it's convenient, or when the patient is in good condition and has a happy chance for a bright future, but always. A doctor promises to give treatment that will sustain life, and euthanasia—no matter how it is practiced—goes directly against that promise.

And there is the final argument, one that many religious organizations support, that life is sacred and holy; that God gives life, and only He has the right to take it away. God alone knows who should die and when. In other words, "Life is a gift in trust (from God), it is on loan, man does not have dominion over it."[15] As long as life persists if we do intervene with the natural processes of dying, we are in a very real way "playing God." "In this view, then, wherever there is human life, any human life, whether comatose life, foetal life, deformed or suffering life, the sanctity of life principle is the final, conclusive reason against taking, ceasing to preserve or (genetically) altering it."[16]

[13] Keyserlingk, *Sanctity of Life,* p. 11.

[14] Ibid., p. 20.

[15] Terry Morris, "Can Death Ever Be Merciful?" *Good Housekeeping,* June 1972, p. 91.

[16] Habgood, "Euthanasia," p. 126.

So the controversy continues. Some believe they have the answers; others live daily with the guilt of either taking a life or of not taking it. For some, life is ended when a doctor walks quietly through a darkened corridor and secretly administers too much pain medication to a patient he has seen suffer agonizingly for months; for others life ends only after months of legal battles waged by family members who are unable to persuade their own doctors to walk that same darkened corridor. We sometimes think that life should never be taken or determined by a physician—until the person lying on the table, writhing in pain, and violated with tubing is our brother, our wife, our infant daughter.

Perspective rules us, and perspectives change. What we believe to be right at one moment we condemn the next. It happens to us all—to doctors, to judges, to juries, to state legislatures, to family members who stand vigil against pain and suffering. And somewhere, sometime, we may learn the answers and come to terms with a difficult problem. We may never solve the complexities of the euthanasia issue; embroiled in legal and moral battles, we may prolong the suffering of thousands. Or we may open the way for thousands to gain a lease on life, to live until a cure is found, to experience love and peace in the dying process.

And through it all, we continue to hope that it will not be us on that stark, white table.

5

ABORTION

Abortion—interrupting and terminating a pregnancy before the fetus or baby can survive outside the mother's body—can result in a crisis, whether the abortion is an accident, as in miscarriage, or is done intentionally. If you are trying to help a woman who is wrestling with abortion, or if you are considering abortion yourself, it is vital that you understand the kinds of emotions involved in terminating a pregnancy.

REASONS FOR ABORTION

Sometimes it's extremely difficult for a woman to find a sympathetic ear if she has decided on the course of abortion. For many, abortion is still unacceptable, and friends and family members may not be able to understand *why* the woman would choose this option. A number of personal, social, or economic reasons may have caused the woman to decide on abortion; some of the most common include the following:

1. The abortion is used as a method of birth control; either the woman did not use birth control or her selected method of birth control failed and she became pregnant.
2. The woman is unmarried and does not want to give birth to an illegitimate child.
3. The woman is unmarried and does not want to be forced into an unwanted marriage.
4. The woman (or couple) already has children and does not want more.
5. The woman (or couple) cannot afford to have the child.
6. The woman wants to hide the fact that she has not been faithful to her husband.
7. The woman wants to avoid parental and community rejection. This is most common with unmarried women.
8. The woman is unmarried and cannot afford the medical expenses associated with the pregnancy and birth.
9. The birth of the child would imperil the well-being of children who already exist.
10. The child will be born into unfortunate circumstances: the mother has a serious or chronic illness, the child will have an inherited defect, the mother is an alcoholic, or the mother is a criminal.

The woman's final decision to seek an abortion depends on many factors; the major ones are her individual psychology, the social pressures she faces, and the willingness of a doctor or clinic to perform the abortion.

In most Western industrial countries most requests for abortions are from single women; in those countries where women marry early and where there are strong family ties most requests for abortion come from married women who already have large families.[1]

While there are many reasons for seeking an abortion there are also some complex reasons why women who might otherwise want an abortion do *not* seek one. An unmarried woman might not seek an abortion because:

1. She is not sure she is pregnant, and she doesn't know how to find out.
2. She is ashamed of the fact that she is pregnant, and she is reluctant to let others know.
3. She doesn't know where to turn for an abortion.
4. The customs in her society dictate total rejection of women who have abortions. Some societies even execute women who have abortions.
5. Her family is willing to support her throughout the pregnancy and after the birth both emotionally and financially.
6. She decides to marry the baby's father or hopes to marry him.
7. Her religious beliefs make abortion an impossible consideration.

[1]*Induced Abortion,* Report of a World Health Organization Scientific Group, (World Health Organization Technical Report Series, no. 623), 1978, pp. 46-48.

8. She wants privacy and anonymity, both of which are difficult to maintain through an abortion.

For married women the main factors keeping them away from abortion include ignorance of where to obtain the abortion, fear of family rejection, and religious beliefs.

ADJUSTMENTS
TO PREGNANCY/ABORTION

One of the things that makes abortion so difficult is that the woman undergoes a realm of changes and adjustments when she becomes pregnant, even if she doesn't want to continue the pregnancy, and then she must make even further adjustments when the pregnancy is terminated.[2] The woman, then, must deal *twice* with the crisis— something you must keep in mind in your efforts to help. Understanding both phases of change and adjustment can help you support the woman as she makes her decision and undergoes the abortion.

Physical and Emotional
Adjustment to Pregnancy

The physical adjustments to pregnancy are well known: the menstrual cycle stops so there is no more menstrual period; the breasts enlarge and become sensitive to touch; the nipples enlarge, darken, and become more prominent; pressure on the bladder causes the need for frequent urination; and there is nausea, sometimes with vomiting, usually in the morning. The woman is usually extremely tired through the first several months of pregnancy.

Even if the pregnancy is not wanted it requires emotional adjustments. The woman must get used to the idea of being pregnant; hostility toward the pregnancy and what it represents is common at first. As the baby grows within the womb and the mother detects movement this hostility may turn to acceptance and feelings of excitement, even if the baby is not wanted. The pregnant woman is unusually receptive to the attitudes of those around her, and she has an increased sensitivity to rejection. Pregnancy usually results in a need for close companionship and for appreciation of the woman.

Physical and Emotional
Adjustment to Abortion

Once the woman makes the choice to have an abortion, or once a miscarriage becomes obvious, she is admitted to a hospital or clinic, is given a physical exam,

[2] This section is based on testimony given before the Royal Commission on Human Relationships by Thomas W. Hilgers, May 21, 1975, in Sydney, Australia.

and undergoes tests including blood tests and cervical culture. She must discuss with the doctor the chosen method for the abortion and must be prepared physically for minor or major surgery, depending on the method.

Before the abortion the woman will feel a strong need for support of her decision; she will need to ventilate her fears and concerns about the abortion, but she will need to talk to someone who is supportive of her decision. She will be unable to concentrate or do her regular work and will feel nervous, tense, and quarrelsome. She may become revolted or upset by her decision. She will find it difficult to tolerate the presence of children and will probably experience upsets in her sexual life.

If the abortion is performed before the woman is eight weeks pregnant her body may not have undergone the changes associated with pregnancy and so it will not have to readjust. If the abortion is performed later, however, the woman will notice that the changes of pregnancy disappear. The nausea and vomiting will disappear, as will the need to urinate frequently. The breasts will regress in size and will lose any tenderness they had; some women will notice a slight milky discharge from the breasts a few days after the abortion.

Regardless of when the abortion was performed the woman may experience cramping, bleeding, and other possible complications, such as infection. Following the abortion, the woman will probably feel that something drastic and dramatic has happened; much to her surprise, she may feel an emptiness and a longing for the baby she has lost. Her emotions may be subtle and may be felt deeply, and it may be extremely difficult for her to express them openly. The woman will probably feel a compelling need to "adjust" quickly to the abortion, but she may experience a "hangover" that corresponds closely to the time that would have elapsed until birth. If the woman is in pain, she will have further emotional reactions.

Factors Intensifying the Emotional Reactions

Regardless of the reactions the woman experiences, certain factors in her life and factors surrounding the abortion itself can intensify the emotions she feels at the time of the abortion and in the months following.[3]

1. *Emotional state before the abortion.*   A woman who is well adjusted and who has a healthy emotional state of mind before the abortion will have less difficulty coping with the abortion than a woman whose emotional balance is precarious to begin with.

2. *Patterns of coping.*   Some women have better regular patterns of coping with any kind of stress than others. Those who have developed patterns of

---

[3]*Hearing before the Subcommittee on Constitutional Amendments: Abortion, Part 2* (Washington, D.C.: U.S. Government Printing Office, 1977), p. 384.

coping that work well for them will be in a better position than those who do not cope well under any kind of stress.

3. *Availability of support systems.* It will be harder to deal with the abortion if the woman is without family members, friends, and others who can help her and support her through the ordeal. A woman who does not have the support she needs from friends and family members may be able to get some support from a professional counselor; however, a woman who does not have access to a counselor will not have as many options.

4. *Situation leading to the abortion.* The woman who is turning to abortion under adverse circumstances—stigma attached to an out-of-wedlock pregnancy, for example—will experience more intense emotional reactions to the abortion.

5. *Perception of the child.* A woman who does not regard the fetus as a child or who views the child as an unwanted financial and emotional strain is less likely to react with guilt and shame than the woman who feels strongly that the fetus is an existing or potential human being. A woman who believes that the child is already existing as a human being can feel like a murderess and can run the danger of experiencing a psychotic breakdown.

6. *Choosing abortion because of fetal deformity.* Surprisingly, a woman or a couple who choose abortion because the fetus is malformed suffer more intense emotional reactions than those whose decision is not based on potential deformity. For some reason, these couples feel that they are somehow responsible for the imperfect child, and their feelings of guilt are usually much more intense and long lasting.

7. *Attitudes of doctors and nurses.* A woman who encounters prejudiced or unsympathetic doctors or nurses during the course of her treatment is likely to suffer prolonged emotional problems related to the abortion.[4] It is important that doctors and nurses who treat an abortion patient learn to give emotional as well as physical support. While a woman who has undergone an abortion should not be housed in a maternity ward she should not be placed in a private room either.

8. *Past mental or emotional illness.* A woman who is suffering from a past emotional or mental illness is at a greater emotional risk. If she wants an abortion and it is denied her emotional state will likely enter a crisis.

Factors that combine to make the abortion a negative emotional experience include the following:

- Strong religious and moral beliefs. The stronger the belief, the more intense the guilt feelings will be.

[4] *Induced Abortion,* pp. 50-53.

- Pressure or coercion from others: boyfriend, clergy, physician, husband, community, family members.
- Feeling that the decision was not the woman's own.
- Lack of counseling from a professional or someone who is qualified to offer counseling.
- Lack of support from family members concerning the decision to have the abortion.
- Degrading or traumatic circumstances surrounding the abortion or the conception of the child, including rape.
- Feelings connecting the abortion with a loss of control over self.
- Poor relationship with the father of the child.
- Poor relationship with members of her own family.
- Physical complications that lead to illness or death.
- Unqualified medical care. The woman who goes to a quack for the abortion will suffer more serious emotional effects.

A woman who underwent a previous abortion and learns that it caused her to miscarry a later, wanted baby also suffers adverse emotional effects. The guilt associated with the miscarriage or premature delivery of a later baby because of an earlier abortion can have devastating effects, leading in some cases to suicide.

HOW CAN YOU HELP?

The most important key in helping a woman who has decided on abortion is to be nonjudgmental. You need to overcome your own feelings regarding abortion, and you need to concentrate instead on helping the woman overcome emotional problems and deal with the feelings she has toward the pregnancy and abortion.

If you can you should offer help to both the man *and* woman involved. Men are not often included in abortion counseling, yet their reactions are often as great as or greater than those of the woman. A man who is not consulted by the woman before she makes the decision to abort a pregnancy often interprets her rejection of the child as a rejection of himself; men often feel left out and isolated in the entire decision-making and resolving process.

It's a myth that men don't care about pregnancy. They need children very much, and they suffer anguish when their child is about to be destroyed. Their feelings of guilt, fright, and aloneness are intensified because the fetus is in the woman's body and the final decision is up to her. Depending upon the state a husband may have no legal right to demand abortion, but neither can he prevent one; legally, the doctor need not even inform the father that the abortion is taking place.

There's another important reason to include the father if you can: abortion has a long-lasting and terrific impact on the couple's sexual and emotional relationship. When Susan became pregnant Larry simply assumed that they would be married; when Susan went ahead with an abortion Larry decided the action was a direct rejection of him, and his depression led to severe emotional illness that destroyed not only his relationship with Susan but his ability to cope with other stresses in his life. If one partner becomes frightened after an abortion and withdraws or walks out of a relationship the other's feelings of rejection and depression increase.

In trying to help a man and a woman who are facing the abortion dilemma remember that you are simply trying to give them advice about alternatives available to them, not advice about abortion as an issue. Help the woman explore her own feelings about the pregnancy, and help the man express his feelings about the pregnancy. Try to create an atmosphere of support, understanding, and nonjudgment. Above all, allow the woman to make her own decision concerning the abortion; *never* force a decision—whether it is to get an abortion or to continue the pregnancy—on the woman or the couple. Once the decision has been made support it and help the woman with whatever she needs.

To be most effective, try to steer away from helping a woman decide whether she wants an abortion; instead, help her explore her own feelings about *why* she wants the abortion. Help her explore the validity of her reasons. Sheila might think that an abortion is her only way out; she realizes she can't pay the medical expenses associated with childbirth even though she might want the baby. In such a situation you might explore with Sheila the sources for funding open to single parents; while you are not forcing her to decide against abortion you are informing her of options and alternatives.

If the woman or couple is undecided you can help them reach a decision by helping them explore four factors.[5]

1. *The woman's life situation.* This includes the woman's relationship with the baby's father. What does the pregnancy mean to him? Was the pregnancy wanted at conception? How does the couple feel about the pregnancy now? Does the mother want to marry the father? How will having a baby affect the woman's life-style and her relationship to the father?

2. *The quality of life available to the infant.* If the pregnancy is continued what kind of life will the infant have? Kim, twenty-two and single, decided on abortion after living with Rachel and her daughter for a year. While Rachel was out dining and dancing, Kim often cared for the two-year-old, whom she did not really like. The baby did not eat well, was often ill, and had emotional problems. Kim couldn't anticipate that life for her own baby would be much better, considering her limited financial circumstances.

Carol, on the other hand, opted to keep her baby. A successful freelance editor, she could work from home, had time and money to spend on the child, which she genuinely wanted.

[5]Cornelia Morrison Friedman, "Counseling for Abortion," in Roberta Kalmar, *Abortion: The Emotional Implications* (Dubuque, Iowa: Kendall/Hunt Publishing Company, 1977), p. 91.

3. *The overall capacity for coping.* How well will the woman, and her family, be able to cope with the pregnancy and birth of the baby? Will the woman be on her own, without help from her family, or will they rally around her, supporting her as the child grows? Does the woman have a good support system that will continue throughout this experience?

4. *The attitude of the woman toward abortion.* An abortion can result in a tremendous crisis if the woman or her family has strong religious or moral beliefs against abortion. A woman who believes she is a murderess is more likely to develop an emotional illness related to the abortion than one who views it merely as a medical procedure.

Try the following techniques when attempting to help the woman or couple considering abortion.[6]

1. *Create a good climate.* Create a climate that is supportive, understanding, and nonjudgmental about the decision to seek an abortion. It is critical that the environment be nonthreatening and that it allow for privacy. Create an environment in which the woman and man are free to ask questions and to express their own feelings without threat of rejection or shock.

2. *Find out what you're working with.* Determine how much knowledge the person already has about abortion; you will probably find out that the person has some misconceptions. Help correct any misconceptions or inaccurate information the person has; if you can, obtain some medical literature that is simple enough for the person to understand. If you need to arrange for the person to talk with a physician who can answer questions regarding procedure and after-effects.

3. *Review the procedure.* You might ask a doctor to help here. Make sure that the woman completely understands the entire procedure; encourage her to ask questions. Ask the doctor to explain thoroughly any medical care—such as injections, intravenous medication, and so on—that will be involved.

4. *Prepare the woman for negative reactions.* Realistically, the woman will probably encounter one or more nurses or nurse aides who will frown on the abortion; the woman should be prepared for this. Talk to her about this kind of rejection and what she will do to cope with it. It may never happen, but she should be prepared for it in case it does.

5. *Review signs of complications.* As with any surgical procedure abortion can lead to complications. Ask a doctor to help you explain these to the woman; let her know which things she should look for after the abortion and what she should do if complications develop. Help the woman feel secure; help her realize that there are people around to help her.

[6]Carolyn Davis, "Abortion Counseling—What We Need to Know and Why," *Journal of Practical Nursing,* June 1975, pp. 16-17.

6. *Provide birth control information.* If the woman is interested provide her with information regarding methods of birth control; you may want to obtain literature on some of these methods. Answer any questions she might have if you can; if necessary ask a doctor or nurse to be present for this discussion.

7. *Discuss alternatives.* The woman may not be aware that she can place her baby up for adoption, or that agencies exist to help her if she chooses to go through with the pregnancy. Don't act as though she *should* choose one of these alternatives but make sure she knows of them.

8. *Write everything down.* As you talk, encourage the woman to write down all the instructions you give; she can use them as a reference later, when she may feel confused or anxious.

ABORTION AND SUICIDE

Although it is always a possibility, suicide is not generally a serious risk among pregnant women. The incidence of attempted suicide among pregnant women is much lower than among the general population, and the number of successful attempts is extremely low.[7] Usually a pregnant woman who attempts suicide is simply trying to make someone realize that she desperately needs help; even then the suicide attempt is usually related to life situations other than the pregnancy and abortion, such as unstable relationships with other family members. Granting an abortion is not usually helpful in preventing the small number of suicides that may take place.

REFUSING TO GRANT AN ABORTION

Even though abortion is legal in the United States a woman who seeks an abortion may be denied it for any of the following reasons:[8]

1. She is a minor and does not have the consent of her parents.
2. The pregnancy has progressed beyond twenty-four weeks, generally considered to be the limit for safety.
3. The woman is mentally disturbed and does not have proper psychiatric counseling.

[7]R. Bruce Sloane, "What Are the Real Emotional Aspects of Abortion?" *Medical Insight,* September 1971, pp. 21-25.

[8]Magda Denes, *In Necessity and Sorrow* (New York: Basic Books, Inc., Publishers, 1976), p. 41.

4. The woman is physically ill and may run a physical risk as a result of the surgery.
5. The woman can't pay for the abortion.

Although a woman cannot physically *need* an abortion in most cases, she may desperately *want* the abortion, and refusal of a doctor to grant the abortion can result in severe emotional stress. Many women seek illegal abortions or go elsewhere for a legal abortion; some authorities feel that a woman who is denied an abortion will not be happy with the baby once it is born. According to statistics unwanted children run a much higher risk of being abused; many suffer economic or emotional deprivation.

Pregnancy presents many physical and emotional changes in a woman's life—changes that require adjustment. Abortion causes even more formidable physical and emotional challenges. As well as the actual surgery or other means chosen for the abortion, other physical changes also occur with the termination of pregnancy. But the emotional upheaval can be even more of a problem to the patient. Women characteristically feel the need for more support and may also feel concerned, fearful, revolted, tense, quarrelsome, nervous, and generally upset (depending upon the reason for the abortion). Thus, those in helping positions need to deal with a woman who is having or has had an abortion with caring and with a nonjudgmental attitude. A woman who is considering an abortion or who has already had one needs someone to help who is skilled in interpersonal relationships and who is able to create an atmosphere of trust and understanding. Remember, abortion is a traumatic experience regardless of the reason behind the termination of pregnancy.

6

CHILD ABUSE

Throughout the centuries and in all societies and cultures children have been abused. Infants have been killed at birth for a host of reasons: to control the population, to eliminate those with defects, to spare their parents the bother of rearing them. Children have been bought and sold, teased and tortured, exhibited and exploited.

There were other kinds of abuse: as recently as this century in this nation children—some as young as three—labored ten to sixteen hours a day in mines, mills, and sweatshops. Prevailing conditions were shocking.

Only recently have we come to realize that children, as well as adults, have rights that must be respected and protected. One of those obvious rights is the right to grow and develop free from physical and mental abuse and free from gross neglect. If they are to become productive, independent human beings who have self-respect as well as esteem for others children must have certain needs met. Those needs should be understood by every person who tries to deal with the difficult problem of child abuse and neglect.

Although it is impossible to isolate a single cause for child abuse a number of factors can combine to cause a parent to lash out at a child; some of these factors include attitudes of society, emotions in the family, individual psychological factors, and a parent's inability to cope with stress.

Society's Attitudes

The use of physical force under some circumstances is sanctioned by society— particularly in the name of protection, law and order, self-defense, and the national interest. Society associates war with manhood. These attitudes sometimes wrongly spill over into family relationships. Physical punishment is widely accepted as a form of discipline, and the Supreme Court has given its blessing on spankings in school. These general attitudes serve to break down barriers that parents may have against physical force or violence.

Family Structure and Roles

The ideal family is characterized by love, affection, emotional support, and gentleness,[1] in reality, every family experiences some conflict among members. These conflicts are normal and result from the normal stresses that come with everyday living. Each family, and each family member, varies in ability to cope with stress once it arises. Some parents, concerned that they resolve their problems in the privacy of their own home, reach a "breaking point"—the only resolution they see is to use physical violence.

Learned Aggression

If aggressive behavior is used and is sanctioned in the home the children will learn to be aggressive. Violence is easily reinforced. If a child stops crying when the parent becomes violent, the parent is encouraged to continue such behavior. Because aggression can be a learned behavior a child who is abused will frequently grow up to abuse his own children.

Common Stress Factors

Stress is involved in everyday living. Some of this stress is chronic—financial instability, unemployment—while other stress can be simply a product of timing.

---

[1] S.K. Steinmetz, *The Cycle of Violence: Assertive, Aggressive, and Abusive Family Interaction* (New York: Praeger Publishers, 1977), p. 3.

At any one time a parent's ability to cope with stress can be reduced by a number of factors. Some of the factors that produce stress most often leading to child abuse include the following:

1. *Geographic isolation.* Families who live in isolated rural areas or who have moved away from family and friends have no personal outlets. Their social supports are few, and they have fewer places to turn in times of stress.

2. *Economic problems.* Money problems can create obvious stresses: poor housing, too little to eat, pressure from creditors. But there are hidden stresses, too: parents, who are expected to be "breadwinners," may suffer a crisis in self-confidence if they are suddenly unable to bring in enough money for their family. This lowering of self-esteem can eventually cause them to turn to violence, which they would not consider under normal circumstances.

3. *Alcohol and drug abuse.* Some feel that alcohol and drug abuse *cause* child abuse; others feel that a parent uses alcohol or drugs as an excuse for violence.

4. *Change in family structure.* Any change in the family structure can cause extreme stress: grandma moves in, the two children from a previous marriage come to stay for the summer, a young child dies. The feelings of anxiety, dependence, fearfulness, and loyalty conflict, resulting in a reduced ability to cope with even small stresses. Even changes in responsibility or role—such as a woman suddenly taking over career responsibility or a man changing jobs—can reduce the ability to deal with stress, leading to the potential for violence.

5. *Medical problems.* Stress results when any family member becomes dependent on other family members because of a medical problem—hyperactivity, mental retardation, physical disability, and so on. A parent suffering extreme stress may not be able to handle a child who is extraordinarily demanding because he can't go out and play with the other children.

6. *Inadequate parenting skills.* Managing children is a big job—and so is being a parent. Too often we take for granted that these skills come as a second nature, but to many they are foreign territory. A parent who does not know how to bathe a baby or discipline a two-year-old will experience stress that can lead to violence if unresolved.

7. *Pregnancy.* Pregnancy can create its own special kind of stress—especially if the child is not wanted, if the mother or father is anxious about being able to provide for the child, or if the father believes the child is not his. Either the mother or the father may take out these stresses and fears on other children in the home, or on the child once it is born.

IDENTIFYING CHILD ABUSE

Abuse of a child may be physical, emotional, or sexual, or the child may simply be neglected. Each type of abuse has its own distinct characteristics that enable you to identify an abused child, but some characteristics are common to all abused children, regardless of the type of abuse.[2]

1. The child appears to be different from other children in physical or emotional makeup; the child's parents may even describe him as being "different" or "bad."
2. The child seems unduly afraid of his parents.
3. The child often has bruises, welts, untreated sores, or other skin injuries. (This will not apply to emotional abuse victims.)
4. The child shows evidence of poor overall care: his clothes are dirty, torn, or poorly fitting; he wears no coat in the winter snow; his teeth are decayed and have not been treated by a dentist; and so on.
5. The child has injuries that seem to be inadequately treated.
6. The child is given inappropriate food, drink, or medication. (Watch the twenty-year-old in the grocery store checkout line who is encouraging a toddler to drink beer from the can.)
7. The child has extremes in behavior. For instance, a child may cry too easily, at the slightest provocation—he gets pushed in line, she drops a toy. Or the child may not cry at all, even when he gets a typhoid shot or falls from a swing.
8. The child is wary of physical contact, especially if it is initiated by an adult. A few abused children may seem hungry for adult affection, and may be inappropriate about how to get it. Lance, seeing an adult approach a small boy who was crying in the park, grew terrified; would that little boy get hit for crying, like he did at home yesterday?
9. The child exhibits a sudden change in general behavior. The little girl next door, who has always seemed so well adjusted, suddenly starts sucking her thumb and pulls all the pansies out of your garden one morning.

HOW YOU CAN HELP

Dealing with child abuse is difficult, because to help the parents you must face the awful reality of violence against children.[3] Your first job is to come to terms with your own feelings about the subject; it is emotionally disturbing to see an

---

[2] National Center on Child Abuse and Neglect, *Child Abuse and Neglect: The Problem and Its Management* (Washington, D.C.: U.S. Department of Health, Education, and Welfare, 1975), DHEW Publication Number (OHD) 75-30073, pp. 4-9.

[3] Adapted from material written for the Office of Child Development by Elizabeth

injured child, and you must resolve your own fears before you can be an effective helper to the parents.

You are in a good position to help such parents—better, in fact, than a doctor or a professional counselor, because abusive parents respond best to other parents or adults who simply try to nurture them. The kind of nurturing you do will, in practice, meet a number of needs these parents have.

1. They need to feel good about themselves. They need to overcome the constant belittling they have experienced throughout their lives. Remember, parents who abuse their children were once abused themselves. You need to help them overcome their feelings of worthlessness.
2. They need to be comforted when they hurt, supported when they feel weak, and liked for their good qualities. Everyone has some good qualities and some bad ones; you need to concentrate on their good ones for a while.
3. They need someone they can trust and lean on. They need someone who will put up with their crankiness. They need someone who will be on time and who will be there in times of crisis. If you say you will be over to take Mary shopping for the afternoon, you'd better be there.
4. They need someone who won't give up, who won't get exhausted with them when they find no pleasure in life. Some parents will do everything they can, seemingly, to defeat you when you try to give them pleasure.
5. They need someone who will help them meet their practical needs. Be willing to make some phone calls, to find out what resources are available in your community. If you don't know the answer to a question be willing to invest some time to find it.
6. They need someone who can appreciate how hard it is for them to have dependent children when they themselves have never been able to be dependent.
7. They need someone who won't criticize them, even when they ask for criticism. They need someone who won't try to tell them how to manage their lives.
8. They need someone who will help them understand their children, without making them feel stupid for not being able to on their own.
9. They need someone who can give to them without making them feel inadequate.
10. They need someone who does not use them in any way.
11. They need to feel valuable. Eventually, they need to be able to help themselves.

The child, too, has needs that must be met; as you work with his parents, keep these needs in mind.

Davoren in 1974 and reprinted from *Child Abuse and Neglect: The Problem and Its Management, Volume 2: The Roles and Responsibilities of Professionals* (Washington, D.C.: U.S. Department of Health, Education, and Welfare, 1975), DHEW Publication Number (OHD) 75-30073, pp. 1-14.

1. He needs to be able to trust someone.
2. He needs to be allowed to be a child.
3. He needs to be encouraged to be an individual.
4. He needs to develop a positive self-image.
5. He needs help in improving the way he interacts with others.
6. He needs help in learning how to communicate his feelings verbally.
7. He needs to learn to control himself; he needs to learn that he can channel aggressive feelings into his play, where he will not harm himself or others.
8. He needs help in learning how to cope with stress.

The needs of the parents are incredible, but what about you? You have to realize that things will be required of you—and you must be prepared to meet these requirements.

1. You need to be extremely sensitive to others.
2. You need to be able to accept hostility or rejection—without being devastated by it, and without needing to retaliate.
3. You need to feel at ease when parents criticize you, yet you can't be critical of the parents.
4. You need to share yourself without sharing your problems.
5. You need to befriend the parents without losing sight of your role as a helper.
6. You need to be able to think first of the parents' needs, not your own.
7. You need to avoid using the parents to increase your own feelings of self-worth.
8. You need a personal sense of achievement and a sight of the goal ahead to lead you through the difficult times.

As you work with the parents remember that they are crying out to have their needs met. Try these specific techniques to help abusive parents.[4]

1. Maintain a neutral, matter-of-fact attitude about the alleged maltreatment. This can be extremely difficult; it is terribly disturbing, even to a seasoned professional, to see a child who has been injured. But you can't react with shock or horror—the parents will turn away from you. You need to be someone they can approach.

2. Keep your attention focused on what the parents tell you, not on what

[4]Robert Borgman, Margaret Edmunds, and Robert A. MacDicken, *Crisis Intervention: A Manual for Child Protective Workers* (Washington, D.C.: U.S. Department of Health, Education, and Welfare, 1979), DHEW Publication Number (ODHS) 79-30196, p. 13; and James W. Lauer, et al., *The Role of the Mental Health Professional in the Prevention and Treatment of Child Abuse and Neglect* (Washington, D.C.: U.S. Department of Health, Education, and Welfare, 1979), DHEW Publication Number (ODHS) 79-30194, pp. 52-54.

you *think* might have happened or what is *obvious*. Something that seems obvious to you might not be the case at all. By refusing to jump to conclusions and by carefully seeking out information from the parents you will earn their trust.

3. Seek information from the parents by asking open-ended questions, questions that can't be answered with a simple "yes" or "no." When the parent gives you an answer repeat it in your own words to make sure you understand, and to demonstrate to the parent that you understand. Restating an answer in your own words also gives the parent a chance to add more information.

4. If you can, talk to the parents separately at first. If Janet's husband is beating her as well as the children she will understandably be reluctant to provide much information in his presence. Talking to the parents separately will enable you to get two different perspectives on the problem.

5. Make it clear that you understand the parents' feelings, but don't condone them. You might say something like, "I can certainly understand why you were so angry with Merrill; it's easy for me to see why you struck him." This kind of communication makes the parent feel at ease and able to communicate more but does not condone the bad behavior.

6. Be supportive whenever you can.

7. Recognize the parents' positive intentions; help them develop some feelings of self-worth. You might say, "I really admire you. It's hard for any of us to admit that we have a problem of any kind. It's really something for you to come here and ask for my help."

8. Recognize feelings and label them for the parents. After Gordon finishes telling you about a confrontation with his son say, "It sounds like you were resentful of Mike" or, "I guess you felt jealous of Mike's success." If you're wrong the parent will correct you, but often the parent has trouble labeling his own feelings.

9. Don't take verbal abuse personally. Remember, these people are in a crisis. You are there, and so you are the one they will yell at.

10. Ask the parents questions about their children. When do they enjoy them most? What is hardest about raising them? What makes them lose control the fastest?

11. Be honest in all your responses to the parents. They can sense pretense and will react with hostile silence.

12. Help the parents develop their support system; help them find ways to involve more people in their lives. Encourage them to contact old friends, or accompany them to an activity. Help parents conquer isolation, either geographic or social.

13. Provide information for parents on what they can realistically expect from their children, but *don't* tell them how to manage their own children. Margie was plunging her one-year-old in scalding water because he wasn't toilet trained; she was surprised to learn that children take much longer to begin toilet training. You might want to invest in a good child development book that is simply written and provides motivation for parents.

14. Help parents develop new interests or hobbies, ways they can productively channel aggression and anger. Jason found new interest in sculpting, while Ann began swimming for sport and exercise.

15. Demonstrate in all you do that you genuinely care about the parents. Keep up contact: make a phone call, drop by to visit, invite them over for a barbecue. Don't drop the ball once the initial crisis has passed.

16. Be a model for child-rearing techniques if the parents ask you to be. You need to be willing to share your techniques for discipline with Alan if he asks you to. Don't be embarrassed, and don't feel that you are on trial. Alan simply needs some new ideas, and he may or may not use some of yours.

17. Encourage the parents to be dependent on you and on others. Often these are parents who were never allowed to be dependent when they were children, and they need this now in their lives.

18. Put the parent at ease while he is talking to you. Maintain good eye contact, sit somewhat forward in your chair to indicate your interest, smile when appropriate, and look relaxed and comfortable. Be aware that even if you are the neighbor on the corner the parents will regard you as an authority figure, and you need to put them at ease as quickly as you can.

As you work with the parents help them set minimal goals for themselves, but don't place heavy demands on them initially. Select goals or help them select goals that are challenging but possible under the circumstances; then praise them for attaining those goals. The key to success in working with abusive parents is to be consistent and dependable. Don't give up; remember, your primary goal is to protect the children involved by helping the parents begin to heal.

7

RAPE AND
SEXUAL ASSAULT

Thousands of women face it each year: rape, one of the most debilitating and unfortunate life crises. Legally, rape occurs when a man has sexual intercourse with a woman without her consent, using force, threats, or fraud.[1]

Rape is a complex situation. The woman is usually physically injured, but there are emotional injuries as well. Her entire life-style will probably be disrupted; she may become pregnant, or she may get venereal disease. And the reactions of those around her may deprive her of all support—her friends may scorn her, she may lose her job, and her husband may even want to divorce her. The woman is completely humiliated by the rapist.[2]

[1] "Precautions Against Rape," *Sexual Behavior,* January 1972, pp. 33-37. Anne Wolbert Burgess and Lynda Lytle Holmstrom, *Rape* (Bowie, Md: Robert J. Brady Company, 1974), pp. 4-15.

[2] Carolyn See, "Rape: No Woman is Immune," *Today's Health,* October 1975, pp. 31-35.

Seven out of ten rapes are committed by someone the victim knows; only 10 percent of those rapes are reported. Half the rapes committed involve the use of a weapon, usually a knife; 10 percent of the rapists inflict injuries so severe that the woman requires medical treatment. About one percent of all rape victims die.

Every nine minutes a woman is raped in the United States;[3] that totals 160 rapes each day, and about 58,400 rapes each year. Rape is the fastest rising crime in the country today.

HOW A WOMAN REACTS TO RAPE

To help a woman who has been raped you need to understand what kinds of reactions she experienced during and after the rape took place.

While most rape victims go into deep shock immediately following the rape certain physical reactions during the rape are common.[4]

1. Struggling and screaming (sometimes just what the rapist wants).
2. Paralysis, sometimes physical, sometimes psychological.
3. Choking, gagging, nausea, vomiting.
4. Pain due to penetration and to physical abuse.
5. Urination.
6. Rapid breathing.
7. Loss of consciousness.
8. Epileptic seizure.

Following the rape, the woman goes through a series of intense emotional reactions that may take months or years to complete; these emotional reactions, considered collectively, are called the *rape trauma syndrome*.

Acute or Impact Reaction

Taking effect immediately and lasting for several days following the rape, the acute or impact reaction phase is a myriad of physical and emotional reactions to the rape itself. The woman is plagued by fear—the fear of how her friends will react, the fear of people not believing her ("I don't have any bruises to prove that I resisted"), the fear of being examined by a male doctor, the fear of reporting the rape, and the fear of the rapist retaliating if she turns him in. And

---

[3] Anne Wolbert Burgess, "The Rape Victim: Nursing Implications," *Journal of Practical Nursing,* November 1978, pp. 20-22.

[4] See, "Rape," pp. 31-35.

there are many other emotional reactions, too: shock, disbelief, agitation, anger, shame, self-blame, confusion, bewilderment, hysteria, and guilt ("Why did I leave the house?").

The woman has specific needs during this stage; chief among them is for others to believe her, even if she seems guilty or if there are no outward signs of a struggle. The woman needs emotional support, acceptance, and reassurance about the way she handled the attack. During this phase the woman should be examined by a physician to establish the rape; you may need to take her to a hospital, and you should be available to help her report the crime if she chooses to do so.

Outward Adjustment Phase

Lasting from weeks to months, the outward adjustment phase is also marked by intense fear—fear of pregnancy or venereal disease, fear of physical violence or death, fear of crowds, fear of being approached from behind, fear of sexual intercourse even with familiar men, and fear of the unexpected. The woman may experience a great deal of anxiety as she anticipates the medical exams that lie ahead or the court hearing, when she must face the rapist, and she may become extremely anxious over the prospect of losing her husband or boyfriend.

Some physical signs are common to the outward adjustment phase. If the woman has been given antipregnancy medication she will be nauseated; she may also suffer nausea, gastrointestinal upset, or loss of appetite even without medication. She may suffer burning sensations when she urinates and may experience an itching or burning discharge from the vagina, which indicates a vaginal infection. As she recovers from bruising and soreness she may experience tension headaches from the emotional tension associated with the rape.

The emotions during this phase range from denial, refusing to believe the rape happened, to loss of a sense of security. The woman may have nightmares or may cry out in her sleep. She will feel overwhelmed by humiliation, embarrassment, self-blame, and feelings of revenge; she will fear sexual things and will experience a disruption of her normal life-style. Any regular problems that she had before the rape will probably be intensified during this phase.

At this point the victim needs you to be patient while she retells the events involved in the rape; even if you've heard them twenty times listen patiently while the woman tells you her story again. She also needs help in approaching her family and friends and will need to have some kind of counseling with her partner so that she can overcome her fear of sexual intercourse. At this phase it is helpful for the woman to meet with other rape victims, in a group if possible, so she won't feel isolated and helpless.

Depression Phase

Lasting for days to months after the rape, the depression phase is marked by obsessive memories of the rape, often occurring during sleep as dreams. The woman will feel a loss of self-esteem as her defenses break down and give way to depression. The woman may express concern about the impact the rape will have on her future life, and she may feel uncertain about being able to control her environment and herself.

The woman needs a great deal of support at this time—support through a divorce, if that happens, and support through the trial and sentencing if the woman decides to prosecute the rapist. Above all, the woman needs to talk, and she needs you to listen, to accept her, to help her resolve her feelings about what happened to her. At this stage she needs to overcome her guilt feelings and she needs help in re-establishing her relationships with men.

Integration and Resolution Phase

The final phase in the rape trauma syndrome, the integration and resolution phase, may take months to years to be completed. The victim at this point has fewer fears—generally simply an avoidance of men and little trust in them—and she has a gradual return to normal sexual activity. She may be fearful of situations that remind her of the rape, and she may feel anxious and depressed when something brings it to mind again.

Again, one of the greatest needs of the victim at this point is to talk, and to have you listen. She also needs the support of others at this time, and should be able to lean on family members and friends for help. As she finally resolves what happened and decides to move on you might encourage her to take some steps to guarantee her security: get an unlisted phone number, move to another house or apartment building, or take an extended vacation to "get away" from the reminders of the rape.

Abnormal Reactions

Normally, the rape trauma syndrome will wind up within a year; if the woman is still behaving abnormally after that time she may be suffering from a compound reaction that will result in permanent damage. Look for these signs.

1. The woman is depressed for an extended period of time.
2. The woman demonstrates psychotic behavior.
3. The woman attempts to commit suicide or talks about committing suicide.
4. The woman becomes an alcoholic or begins abusing drugs.

5. The woman starts acting out the rape scene.

6. The woman turns to lesbianism when she was previously heterosexual.

7. The woman expresses a hatred of sex.

This kind of abnormal reaction is more likely to take place in a victim who was disturbed before the rape—a woman who was physically ill, emotionally ill, or who had social difficulties. If you see a pattern of these signs developing you should arrange for the woman to receive professional help immediately.

HELPING THE RAPE VICTIM RECOVER

Most of the flurry of activity immediately following the rape will be conducted by doctors, nurses, social workers, or police—people who need to gather evidence for an arrest or who need to treat the victim's physical injuries. As a friend or family member you won't have a great deal of input during the hours immediately following the attack.

It's later—days, weeks, or months after the rape—when your support can be instrumental in helping the rape victim recover from the experience. Like any other crisis in life a rape can result in a growth experience for the victim *if* she is handled properly and given the amount of support she needs during a difficult time.

Relating to rape victims and coping with the aftermath of a shattering experience is a very sensitive matter. Your attitudes will have a great impact on the victim and her perception of herself. Believe in the victim, and show her that you believe in her; let her tell you her side of the story, and do your best to understand.

Some specific principles can help you in dealing with a rape victim:[5]

1. Deal with your own feelings and reactions first; you need to be under control before you can help someone else.

2. Let the victim know you are available for help, but know your own limitations. Keeping your limitations in mind you might give the victim your phone number, offer to call her at a certain time, or offer to let her stay with you in your home.

---

[5]Dorothy Backer, "Advice on Counseling a Rape Victim," *Practical Psychology for Physicians,* January 1975, pp. 35-41; Anne Wolbert Burgess and Lynda Lytle Holmstrom, "The Rape Victim in the Emergency Ward," *American Journal of Nursing,* 73, no. 10 (October 1973), pp. 1740-45; Ann Wolbert Burgess and Lynda Lytle Holmstrom, "Rape Trauma Syndrome," *American Journal of Psychiatry,* 131:9 (September 1974), pp. 981-86; Charles R. Hayman and Charlene Lanza, "Victimology of Sexual Assault," *Medical Aspects of Human Sexuality,* October 1971, pp. 152-61; John Stratton, "Rape and the Victim: A New Role for Law Enforcement," *FBI Law Enforcement Bulletin,* November 1975, pp. 3-6; "Injuries Incurred During Rape," *Medical Aspects of Human Sexuality,* March 1976, pp. 77-78.

3. Support the woman, but don't make decisions for her. Instead, let her know that the decisions are hers to make and that you will support her in whatever she decides.

4. Encourage the woman to report the rape to the police—but understand that she will be reluctant from wrongly believing that she somehow "asked" for the rape; embarrassment in anticipation of the pelvic examination; or fear that the rapist may retaliate if she reports the incident. Remember that it takes a great deal of courage to report a rape and then look forward to reliving the incident for months to police, juries, and judges.

5. If the woman decides not to report the rape after you have encouraged her to do so, respect her decision. *Never* report the rape for her when she has decided not to.

6. Work slowly and carefully. Your immediate reaction is important, and you need to take time to determine the victim's emotional state of being. Let her give you the facts, and don't impose your own feelings on her at this time.

7. A woman who has been raped will feel helpless; the best way to combat this is to *do* something. If she has decided to report the rape help her phone the police; if she has decided not to report the rape help her change her clothing and clean up.

8. Don't surround the woman with silence or reproach; you may confirm her worst suspicions, that she is guilty of some terrible wrongdoing and that the rape is her "fault."

9. Never blame the victim for the rape.

10. Never blame yourself for the rape. Perhaps you have decided that if you hadn't left your children with a sitter your daughter would not have been raped; maybe you think that your wife wouldn't have been raped if you had let her take the car to her friend's house. Overcome these feelings—the rape is not your fault, any more than it is the woman's fault.

11. The woman may get angry and may displace her anger on you, shouting at you, swearing at you, or attempting to strike you. Don't take this personally, even if her attack seems very personal; she needs someone to vent her anger on, and if you're there for her she'll choose you. Conquer your desire to retaliate; continue to treat her with empathy and kindness.

12. Don't berate the woman for her situation, and don't dwell on things that are beyond her control—"If you had moved to a safer apartment this whole thing wouldn't have happened," or "If you didn't have a night job you wouldn't have gotten raped." There are two things wrong here: first, you make the woman feel responsible and guilty for the rape; second, the woman can't change what has already happened and maybe couldn't change the circumstances anyway (maybe she *had* to work at night to make ends meet).

13. Don't dwell on the sexual aspects of the rape. It will be extremely difficult for the woman to re-establish her regular and normal sexual relationships anyway, and dwelling on the sexual part of the rape will just reinforce the woman's feelings of alienation.

14. Offer unconditional, nonjudgmental affection. Physical acceptance will help the woman overcome feelings of loneliness. You might touch her hand, pat her arm, or put your arm around her shoulders. Some rape victims feel "dirty" and "unworthy" of being cared for.

15. The woman will probably need to tell her story many times over to you— let her. Listen with patience, letting her retell every vivid detail as many times as she needs to. At first, her accounts will be packed with emotion and will include sexual details; as she tells the story again and again she will gain better control over her emotions and will not find it necessary to be as explicit. Listen carefully to the story each time she tells it, and tell her you do not mind hearing it again. Never act bored or impatient.

16. As you work with the woman you might need to offer support to other family members, especially her husband, who may be feeling some combination of rage and guilt. Reinforce his feelings, help him know that it is acceptable to feel that way, and emphasize that he was in no way responsible for what happened. Remember that a hysterical family member may lash out at you, just as the victim might; be prepared for such attacks, and don't take them personally.

17. As the woman works through her feelings in the days and months following the rape make sure that she doesn't start attaching too many emotional problems or unresolved life conflicts to the rape. A woman who has always had problems in her interpersonal relationships, for instance, needs to accept that she has always had a problem instead of falling back on the excuse that she was raped. If you can see that the woman is using the rape as a sort of crutch you may need to refer her to professionals for help.

In addition to the above general principles you may need to treat a woman a little differently because of her life situation or her age.

A woman with children needs help in figuring out how to tell her children what happened to her. The woman is usually concerned that her children will suffer some social stigma. While the woman wants to impress upon her children the dangers associated with walking alone, talking to strangers, and so on, she does not want to breed an unhealthy fear in them. You should help the woman by listening to her concerns and by helping *her* formulate a plan for telling the children; again, the ideas should be hers; you help by actively listening and reinforcing. She may want you to be there when she tells them; if she does respect her wishes and arrange to be with her. It is important for children to see, firsthand, that even though their mother went through a terrible ordeal she is fine now, but she will require some extra love and understanding.

A divorced or separated woman is in a particularly difficult position. She is more likely to be blamed—"She *asked* for that!" She is more likely not to be believed. Her life-style, her morality, and her character are often questioned. Because of the reactions of those around her the woman sees the rape as a confirmation of her inadequacies. Very few divorced or separated women report a rape because they don't want to be blamed, ridiculed, or questioned.

For this woman it is extremely important that you believe her. Come right out and tell her that you believe her, and then give her verbal reinforcement as she tells you the story of the rape: "That must have been horrible!" "You must have been frightened then," "What kind of a car was the man driving?" Your comments and questions will let her know that you are taking her seriously and that you believe what she is telling you.

This woman is also in another unique position: her independence is critical to her life-style, and that independence has been threatened by the rape. Do whatever you can to encourage the woman to remain independent; encourage her to do many things for herself. Give her support in overcoming her fears so that she can continue to live alone.

Single young women often feel guilty and blame themselves for not being more assertive in fighting the rapist; even women who were threatened with a gun or a knife often feel they could have done more. Help her realize that she could not have been expected to do more than she did; a rapist chooses as a victim a woman who is helpless. A rapist will never choose a woman he thinks can fight.

If the rape is the young woman's first sexual experience you will need to talk carefully during the weeks and months that follow the rape so that she will be able to separate the sexual from the violent aspects of the rape. Let her know that some things that happened during the rape—orgasm, fondling, and so on—are perfectly natural and are even desirable when experienced in a loving way under circumstances she chooses with a partner she cares for. This kind of counsel is critical. Later, when the woman experiences orgasm during sexual intercourse, she may have renewed feelings of guilt and reproach if she has not been able to successfully separate the two.

If the victim is particularly young or inexperienced she may not be able to tolerate the gynecological examination following the rape; she may view it as a second rape. If you sense that the girl is having this kind of problem you may suggest to the physician that she be heavily sedated before he begins the exam. Stay with her through the exam, or arrange for a trusted and loved family member to be there with her.

As with a divorced or separated woman a young single woman's independence is critical to her—she has fought hard for it, and with the rape she may suddenly see that everyone wants to "take care of" her again. Encourage the young woman in all ways to be as independent as she can; reassure her that having a friend to talk to is not a sign of weakness or dependence.

The road to recovery from rape is a long, hard one; but those who have support from friends and family members are much more successful in traveling the road. You can be the key that helps a rape victim unlock her future and go on with her happy, productive life.

PSYCHIATRIC EMERGENCIES

You receive a telephone call one afternoon from a neighbor; she tells you that there seems to have been a violent disturbance in the house on the corner, and she asks for your help.[1] It could be a simple marital spat, grandad on a rampage (confused, as usual), a jealous lover, or murder. As you rush to the house you realize that there may be some physical injuries and that it may be necessary to call for medical help, but you also realize that there will be some mental problems, too—at least one person who is uncooperative, tearing the house apart, yelling.

When you arrive at the house and approach the front door you hear glass breaking and a lot of shouting. Beth, a tired and disheveled forty-two-year-old woman, is waiting at the door.

Your first course of action? Ask Beth what happened or is still happening.

---

[1]The example is adapted from Benjamin H. Glover, "The Acutely Disturbed Patient and His Family," *Emergency Medical Services,* November/December 1975, pp. 38-40.

Get a history. Don't try for a detailed history, of course, but find out briefly what has happened and what the situation is now. Ask her if anyone is hurt and how severe the injury is. If you find out that there is an injury of some sort call for medical help if Beth or someone else has not already done so; do not go into the house, but use a neighbor's phone or ask the neighbor to call. Especially if you find out that there is raw anger—that there is an uncontrolled, belligerent, attacking person inside, who is still thrashing around and throwing things—send for help. Don't go into the house alone.

While you are waiting for help to arrive get more history. Ask Beth to come out on the front lawn with you. Ask her if the belligerent man—in this case her husband, Keith—has been drinking alcohol, has had any recent illnesses or has taken any medication lately, either prescription or illegal. Ask her if Keith has recently lost his job or undergone any other recent stress. Has he hit his head? Has he ever acted like this before? While you wait for help, then, try to figure out why he might be acting like he is. Take mental note of any information you might be able to provide medical authorities when they arrive.

Quickly assess Beth for any physical injuries; if she has them stay with her until medical help arrives, or perform first aid if you are trained. If her injuries are slight or if she has no injuries ask her to lie down on the front lawn and rest quietly.

When your helpers arrive—medical help, social service help, or other neighbors—find out from Beth which room her husband is in and how to get there. Take your helpers and move quickly to the room where Keith is; close doors behind you as you move toward him.

As soon as you get into the room where Keith is close the door and form a circle around him. Be calm and silent. Present a firm atmosphere, but try not to be threatening. Look at him closely, and try to determine what has happened.

The first priority is to have any physical injuries treated; the medical personnel you summoned can take care of this. If there are children or other family members in the room their injuries should be treated and they should be quietly taken from the room, where they can wait outside with Beth.

Once Keith's injuries have been treated establish communication with him. This should be done by *one* person—you. Use his name repeatedly as you speak to him in a clear, slow voice.

Tell him your name, who you are, and that you want to talk to him. Even if he knows you, you should repeat this information. Don't shout at him, order him around, or lose control yourself. Your dialogue might go something like this:

"Hello, Keith. My name is John Smith; I live in the red brick house on Yalecrest. I'm here to help you. I don't want to hurt you in any way. I just want to talk to you."

You need to take care of your own feelings at this point—make sure they are under control. If there is anything about the situation that is making you uncomfortable, or if you feel incapable of dealing with the man, resolve it now.

"Keith, please put that gun down so I can talk to you. I'm sorry, but I can't talk to you while you are holding the gun. If you will put it down on this chair, I promise you that no one will touch it. Thank you, Keith. I feel better now, and I can talk to you now. I want to try to understand why you are so angry."

Don't make promises you can't keep—don't use any trickery. Be completely straightforward and honest. Don't give the person any reason to mistrust you or to lose control of his emotions again. Above all, remain calm. Keith may panic anew if he feels you aren't in control either. Make sure that your helpers remain quiet and controlled in the background. *You* are the person who is establishing communication; the helpers should not attract attention to themselves in any way unless they are needed to restrain a sudden physical outburst.

As you talk to Keith try to find out why he was acting like he was. Use the "go-along" technique; go along with what he tells you, but set some definite guidelines as to how you want him to act:

"I understand how you might feel that all these neighbors are here to hurt you. You might even think that I am here to hurt you. You must be frightened. I can see how you are troubled about these people, but they won't try to hurt you at all, Keith. They are friends of mine. I won't try to hurt you, either. We all want to help you, Keith. Come with me now, Keith. That's the best way to handle this. I'll stay with you, Keith. I will not let anyone hurt you."

As you talk to the person use one-thought sentences. Keep talking as you move; try to get the person to move with you by the things you say.

If the person suddenly becomes violent it is essential that he be restrained. *Never use leathers, cuffs, blankets, or ropes.* Restrain the person by simply outnumbering him. Your helpers should move in quickly and simply restrain him; you should make this procedure clear to everyone before you go into the house. Make sure beforehand that the helpers understand that they are not to strike the man or do anything that will harm him physically; they are simply to form a wall around him and force him to submit. They should not shout, threaten, or even speak. If the violence continues you may have to ask a medical professional to sedate the man and move him to a hospital.

"Keith, I know you're upset." Speak calmly. Don't shout. "I know you're angry, Keith. I want to help you. I know that you are afraid now. I want to help you by calming you down. We will take you to a place where you can be cared for better than here. Will you please lie down on the bed, and let me sit here next to you? One of my friends will give you an injection that will help calm you. Then we can work together so you will no longer be afraid."

Keith may lie down voluntarily. If he does not your dialogue may go something like this:

"If you want to stand up, that's all right. Just make sure that you don't hit any of these friends who are here to help you. I don't want to fight you, but I don't want you to run away or hurt yourself. Will you please roll up your sleeve so my friend can give you this injection? I will need to hold your arm steady, but I will not hurt you. My friend will not hurt you either, Keith. Please do not hit us, Keith. Everything is all right. I am going to hold your arm now, and my friend is going to give you your medicine. Then we will go to a place where you will be more comfortable than you are here. Thank you for your help, Keith."

Monotonous repetition is helpful. If this approach does not help the first time, repeat it. It might take you thirty minutes to calm the man down; even if it does it is better than getting gouged eyes, bruises, pulled hair, broken bones, or a gunshot wound.

This example provides a general guideline of how to deal with an emotionally disturbed person. It is critical that you work quickly, effectively, and properly so that you can save lives without further injury. The ability to recognize mental and psychiatric emergencies and your knowledge of their treatment and management will help you understand how best to render psychiatric first aid and how to manage psychiatric emergencies.

PRINCIPLES OF MANAGEMENT

A number of general guidelines can help you best deal with a person presenting a psychiatric emergency:[2]

1. Be prepared to spend time with the victim. Many times you must be able to take the time to talk to the victim and learn what is bothering him; in many cases diagnosis without such time investment is impossible. Some psychiatric disorders stem from severe suspicion of others; if you act hurried or panicked the victim may decide that you are trying to hurt him, and he may strike out at you or attempt to escape.

---

[2] List compiled from C.J. Frederick, "Emergency Mental Health," published by Brent Q. Hafen and Keith J. Karren, *Pre-Hospital Emergency Care-Crisis Intervention* (Denver: Morton Publishing, 1981), p. 467, pp. 10-13, 18-26; Gilbert M. Hefter, "Psychiatric Emergencies," *Emergency Medical Services,* September/October 1974, pp. 13-18; Jack Zusman, "Recognition and Management of Psychiatric Emergencies," *Emergency Psychiatric Care* (Bowie, Md.: Charles Press Publishers, Inc., 1975), pp. 42-57; Stephen Soreff and Patricia Olsen, "Emotional Emergency," *Emergency Medicine,* October 1975, p. 233; Robert A. Matthews and Lloyd W. Rowland, *How to Recognize and Handle Abnormal People* (Arlington, Va.: National Association for Mental Health, 1954), pp. 8-17; National Highway Traffic Safety Administration, "Management of the Emotionally Disturbed," (Washington, D.C.: U.S. Department of Transportation, 1977, DOT Publication Number HS 501207; and Mark G. Shub, "Management of the Psychiatric Patient," *Emergency Medical Technician Journal,* 1, no. 4, pp. 70-71.

2. Be as calm and direct as possible. Most emotionally disturbed individuals are terrified of losing self-control; you will elicit the best response and cooperation if the victim has confidence in your ability to maintain control of yourself and the situation. If you manifest anxiety or panic you will only further convince the victim that the situation is overwhelming or hopeless.

3. Identify yourself clearly. Tell the victim exactly who you are and what you are trying to do for him. Many victims are confused and upset and will not trust you unless you are explicit in your instructions.

4. Don't rush the victim off to the hospital immediately unless there is some medical emergency that needs prompt attention. Keep the victim at the scene as long as possible, it may offer clues as to why he is acting as he is. A victim who is hysterically rushed to a hospital will have his suspicions that something is terribly wrong strengthened.

5. Interview the victim alone even if you know that later you will have to get other details from family members or friends. Ask family members and friends to go to another room where your partner or helpers can ask them questions about the victim. The victim should stay with you, and you should guarantee him that he has privacy and that you respect his right to that privacy. Many times a victim will hesitate to talk in front of relatives or friends because he is ashamed of his problems and does not want to lose respect in their eyes; other times they may be the source of the problem—a fact he couldn't divulge in their presence.

6. Sit down with the victim while you interview him; never tower above him. Most victims of psychiatric disorders have problems relating to others, especially authority figures, and many have become suspicious and distrustful; you will get the best results if you do everything you can to relate to the victim and to put yourself on his level. He needs to trust you before he can confide in you.

7. Let the victim tell his story in his own way. Don't attempt to direct the conversation by asking the victim questions that really have nothing to do with what he is trying to tell you. Let him ventilate all of his feelings if he appears willing to do so—that in itself can be therapeutic. If you can offer him a cigarette or a cup of coffee or a soft drink; these will help promote a more relaxed atmosphere.

8. Be interested in the victim's story and empathize, but don't be over-sympathetic. If you overwhelm him with pity he may decide that his situation is indeed hopeless. Treat him as if you expect him to improve and to recover; let him know that you expect him to feel better soon, even though you know that he is having problems now and you can understand why.

9. Never be judgmental. The victim is convinced that his feelings are accurate—they are real to him, no matter how ridiculous they may appear to you.

Accept his right to have his own feelings, and don't blame him for feeling the way he does. Above all, don't criticize him for his feelings.

10. Be honest with the victim. Reassure him sincerely; give him supportive information that is truthful. Tell the victim what you expect from him, and tell him what he can expect from you. Then make sure you follow through. Don't make any promises that you can't keep.

11. Take a definite plan of action. This technique helps reduce the victim's anxiety.

12. Don't require the victim to make decisions. For instance, don't say, "Would you like to go to the hospital?" Instead, say in a firm but kind voice, "I think it is important that you go with me to the hospital. There are doctors there who can help you to feel better about things." Victims of psychiatric disorders have often lost their ability to cope effectively, and presenting them with the dilemma of having to make a decision can further overwhelm them, even if the decision is a simple one.

13. Encourage the victim to participate in some motor activity; this further reduces anxiety. If you decide to transport the victim to the hospital, for instance, let him gather up the things that he will need, and let him tidy up the apartment or house or water the plants before you leave. Let him do as many things for himself as he can—this will help restore his confidence in himself and lessen his feelings of helplessness and hopelessness. If physical problems make it necessary for medical personnel to transport the victim go with him to the hospital.

14. Stay with the victim at all times. Once you have responded to the emergency the victim's safety is legally your responsibility. Even if he pleads to be left alone for a few minutes firmly explain to him that you realize he is capable of handling things himself but that you could get fired if you leave him alone. The friend should not do all the talking. One of the most important things a friend can do in a psychological emergency is to allow the victim to ventilate his feelings without judgment or criticism. Expressing feelings not only helps ventilate them but puts them in perspective. Friends might also help explore alternatives.

15. Never assume that it is impossible to communicate with a victim until you have tried. Family members or friends may tell you not to waste your time because they have all tried to talk to the victim; the victim, however, may be unable to discuss his problem with a friend or a family member and may, instead, prefer to talk to you.

16. Ask the victim questions that are direct and specific. This will enable you to measure his level of consciousness and his contact with reality. Don't confuse him by asking him questions that are too complicated or that may further confuse him.

17. If a victim is extremely fearful or violent skip the attempt to find out if something is physically wrong with him. If you try to examine him physically or if you authorize a medical official to do so you may only increase his panic.

18. As you interview the victim don't be afraid of silence. The silences may seem intolerably long, but maintain an attentive and relaxed attitude. If the victim has stopped speaking because he is overwhelmed by emotion it is especially critical that you refrain from speaking. Don't try to forestall the victim's emotional expression; for instance, don't try to distract him to keep him from crying. Victims of psychiatric disorders need to express emotion even though it may be hard for them.

19. As you talk to the victim encourage him to communicate by gestures (such as a nod of the head) or by verbal response (such as "I see," or "Go on"). Always be careful to let the victim know that you are interested in what he has to say and that you would like to learn more.

20. As you interview the victim point out something in his behavior or conversation that will help you direct the conversation in ways helpful to you. Do this only if the victim seems to be wandering aimlessly; never interrupt the victim while he is trying to express a thought or trying to tell you about something. If the victim has nothing to say you can direct the conversation by saying something like, "You seem worried," or "You sound very angry." Make sure that your comments are not condescending or nagging.

21. Make sure that your questions are nondirective. (Don't guide the person into an answer where little information is given. The person should be encouraged to express their feelings.) Avoid asking questions that can be answered with a "yes" or "no."

22. Don't foster unrealistic expectations in the victim. For instance, don't listen to his story and then say, "You have nothing whatsoever to worry about." Instead, find out what the victim's strengths are, and then reinforce them. You might say, "Despite all of the problems you have had you seem to have done very well at work."

23. Respect the victim's personal space. Some victims will be able to tolerate you if you sit close to them and touch them; others, even when they are not disturbed, prefer to maintain a distance and don't like to be touched.

24. Don't abuse or threaten the victim. A victim of a psychiatric emergency is already frightened; he might even be hearing voices. He can't stand the thought of one more person trying to hurt him. He needs a friend. If you treat him in a way that further threatens him he may become convinced that you are going to hurt him. At that point he will either resist help or will try to prevent you from approaching him, usually by violence.

25. Don't let the victim get your goat. Many victims of psychological disorders are irritable and are adept at picking out your weaknesses; they may feel threatened themselves, and they may try to improve their situation by belittling you. It is important that you remain kind and calm. You may be upset by what the victim says to you, but do not react in any way. He is ill, and his comments are not directed against you personally. Help him through his problems and help him regain his self-confidence; the insults will cease.

26. Avoid any kind of excitement. If the victim has attracted a crowd either move the victim to a quiet place or ask helpers to get rid of the bystanders. Once you have the victim alone do everything possible to keep a crowd from forming.

27. If the victim is severely disturbed and has become violent it will be necessary for you to restrain him. Never attempt physical restraint alone; wait until helpers have arrived before you begin the restraint attempts. Don't be ashamed to call for help. Use only as much force as is absolutely necessary to restrain the victim; don't bully him in any way.

28. If the scene of the accident or the environment is especially hectic remove the victim before you try to calm him. Don't take him a long distance; you just need to go into another room, across the street, or out into the yard.

29. Once you have figured out what the victim's problem is make every attempt to explain it fully to him and to explain to him that he can be helped, and to tell him what the probable outcome will be. Don't try to frighten him, but be honest in letting him know what will be done to help him. Many times a victim may be more anxious and fearful because he is uncertain about what is going to happen to him now that you know what is wrong with him.

30. Communicate confidence in yourself. This needn't be done verbally—instead, move with assurance and calm.

31. Once the person has told you his whole story go back over it briefly with him to make sure that you understand what he said and that you didn't misinterpret anything.

32. If the victim disagrees with you don't argue with him. Instead, point out that there are many different ways to interpret a situation; admit that you might be wrong, and tell him that he is free to agree or disagree. If you are uncertain about how the victim might react to a statement keep quiet.

33. As soon as possible contact family members and friends who might know what has happened to the victim. Don't confine yourself to only the victim's close friends or family members; sometimes a casual acquaintance who lives down the street can provide missing information that those closer to the victim might have overlooked or considered trivial.

34. Find out if the victim has been treated for a psychological or physical disorder before the present emergency. Contact the former therapist; you might want to consider transporting the victim to the therapist instead of to the hospital.

35. Make detailed notes about everything you learn about the victim for medical as well as legal reasons.

36. Never leave the victim alone; consider all psychiatric emergency victims to be escape risks, even if they are acting calm and undisturbed.

37. Provide the victim with ordinary comforts; allow him to get a drink of water, go to the bathroom, have some food to eat, and get on dry clothing if he is wet. If you let him go to the bathroom make sure that he can't escape through a window. You may have to ask someone to stand outside the window and watch.

38. A victim of a psychiatric emergency should only be given tranquilizers as a last resort.

39. Try to get the victim to go to sleep; sleep often helps restore psychological equilibrium.

40. If you choose to leave the victim at his home be careful to quell any rumors about him. Tell the family in clear terms exactly what is wrong, what has happened, and what the outcome will be. Tell them that rumors and gossiping about the victim can hurt him immeasurably if he should happen to overhear them.

41. If the victim is a child deal with issues indirectly, since the child may be unable to talk about problems directly. You might be able to work around to the problem through techniques such as storytelling, game playing, or picture drawing.

42. Give a victim who is a child some food: a cookie or a favorite candy bar or a piece of fruit.

43. Make an interview with a child short; his attention span will be short.

44. Never lie to a child. If you have to tell him something unpleasant do it gently and gradually.

45. If the victim is paranoid explain all your actions carefully and clearly before you do anything. Let the victim ask you questions if he needs to. Answer all questions fully and clearly even if they seem trivial to you.

46. If the victim is paranoid make sure he is unarmed before you start the interview.

47. If the victim is paranoid don't try to be friendly or informal. Paranoid individuals often misinterpret attempts at friendliness as an effort to subvert them instead. Maintain some distance, and act in a businesslike manner without being brusque or rude. Don't grant the victim special considerations or privileges; he will misunderstand and suspect you of trying to win him over so you can harm him more easily. If the victim clearly requests a special privilege and fully explains why it is necessary to him you may go ahead and grant it.

48. If a paranoid person suddenly becomes aggressive or hostile restrain him firmly. A paranoid person may become extremely dangerous, and he should never think that he can overcome you.

49. If the victim is armed and barricaded negotiate with him. Convince him that you are not there to hurt him, that no harm is intended, and that you are *not* a police officer. Tell him that you know he is suspicious and that he should tell someone about those suspicions. Tell him you are there to listen to him and to enlist help for him. If he still does not respond isolate him and wait for him to become hungry or thirsty.

50. If the person is a victim of violence encourage him to wash, take a soothing bath, or change clothes so that he can be more comfortable. Consult police officers quickly so that they can gather pertinent information. Washing should only be done after evidence has been gathered and cleared by the police.

51. If the person is a victim of amnesia approach him slowly and cautiously; tell him you are there to help him, and offer him something to eat or drink. Make a few attempts to jog the person's memory, and if the victim is lost begin to mention landmarks and places that are nearby. Especially if the victim is elderly, you can safely assume that he hasn't walked far.

Above all, don't hesitate to call for medical help. If you are not able to work successfully with a mentally disturbed person medical personnel may be able to drive him to a hospital or state or county mental health center, where he can receive professional help in overcoming his problems.

DEPRESSION

Depression, the blues, depressive illness—whatever you choose to call it, it is one of the most common and oldest of all medical disorders. Descriptions of the disease are found sprinkled throughout literary history, including the Bible. Today, in the United States alone, 125,000 people are hospitalized each year for depression, and more than 200,000 receive outpatient treatment.[1]

What is depression? By definition, it is a group of emotional disorders ranging all the way from brief periods of mild dejection to incapacitating illness that can result in suicide.

Depression is a normal and natural emotion; in fact, we would be abnormal if we could not feel this emotion in the form of grief during very stressful periods of life—loss of employment, death in the family, or some other loss. Most of us recover quickly from these periods of sadness, but a significant num-

[1] "The Pervasive Problem of Mental Depression," *Medical World News*, April 20, 1973, pp. 42-48.

ber of people seem extremely vulnerable to stress. About 15 percent of the people in America between the ages of eighteen and seventy-four suffer from a disease known as clinical depression; they are unable to deal with these normal feelings of sadness and overcome them.[2]

Depression is an underlying factor in many physical illnesses; it can also lead to drug addiction, alcoholism, suicide, and some forms of social deviance, including homosexuality. Because of its widespread effects depression is considered to be a major health concern for all society.

The causes and appearance of depression are different at different times of life. Depression occurs more often in middle or old age than in youth; about 8 percent of men and 16 percent of women can expect to suffer from a depressive illness during their lifetime.[3] Major depression is a recurrent illness, too; if you suffer it once, you have an 80 percent chance of suffering it again at some time in your life.

SIGNS AND SYMPTOMS OF DEPRESSION

A variety of symptoms can indicate depression, and these symptoms differ depending on the person's age and emotional health. However, some signs and symptoms are characteristic of all grades of depression.[4]

SPECIFIC MOOD CHANGES   These mood changes can be anything from mild sadness to intense, distressing misery, usually accompanied by feelings of hopelessness, despair, and loneliness. People who suffer mood changes can become extremely self-concerned; some want to die, and some actually consider suicide. Many people feel worse in the morning and improve toward the evening.

OVERALL CHANGE IN ACTIVITY AND LEVEL OF THINKING   The person may become agitated and may experience a general slowdown in thinking, including a slowdown in the ability to concentrate or make decisions.

NEGATIVE SELF-CONCEPT   A negative self-concept includes feelings

---

[2]Virginia, Rosslyn, *Depression, The Thin Edge* (National Association for Mental Health, 1973), p. 3.

[3]*Depression* (New York: Medcom, Lakeside Laboratories, Inc., 1970), p. 8.

[4]W.L. Parry-Jones,"Masked Depressive Illness," *Update International,* April 1974, p. 239; and Donald H. Naftulin, "Detection and Management of Depression," *Continuing Education for Physicians,* March 1974, p. 27.

of self-blame, self-reproach, and feelings of failure; the person may want to punish himself.

LOSS OF INTEREST   Work, home life, and relationships are less compelling. The person lacks energy and may feel the need to escape and hide. The more serious the depression is, the more unpleasant it is to be around the person, and the more likely it is for others to attempt to ignore his problems.[5]

Depression is usually considered serious according to the duration, rather than the intensity, of the illness. A person who is depressed mildly for a year, for instance, is considered to be in greater trouble than a person who is deeply depressed for a week or two.

General Symptoms of Depression

PHYSIOLOGICAL SYMPTOMS	EMOTIONAL SYMPTOMS	PSYCHIC SYMPTOMS	BEHAVIORAL SYMPTOMS
Chronic fatigue	Sadness, the blues	Inability to concentrate	Loss of function
Inability to sleep	Crying		Withdrawal from activity
Early awakening	Lack of feeling	Loss of interest in family events	
Headaches	Apathy toward social life or hobbies	Poor memory	Psychomotor retardation
Loss of appetite			Lack of attention to grooming routines
Weakness and fatigue	Anxiety	Suicidal thoughts	
Loss of sex drive	Feelings of failure	Lack of enjoyment	
Menstrual changes	Delusions of guilt, self-reproach	Failure to feel rested after sleep	Behavior excesses
Nausea			Initiation of fewer interpersonal behaviors
Sudden weight loss (or gain)	Fears of physical illness		
Dizzy spells	Chronic unhappiness		Focus of behavior toward one person
Gastrointestinal upsets	Loss of self-esteem		
Dryness in the mouth	Irritability, hostility		
Indigestion	Fears of various kinds: of insanity, loneliness, changing jobs, moving		
Constipation			
Dyspepsia			
Heart palpitations			
Slowing speech and movements			

[5] R.W. Burgoyne and R. Bruce Sloane, "Depression," *Continuing Education for Physicians,* December 1976, p. 28.

DEPRESSION IN CHILDREN

Until recently it was thought that only adults suffered from depression; now we realize that infants and children are capable of suffering from depression, although their symptoms vary from those experienced by adults.

Depression in children can be caused by a physical defect or illness; malfunction of the endocrine glands; mental retardation; mismanagement of the child during infancy; poor discipline; lack of affection, causing the child to feel insecure; lack of encouragement for achievements; failure to gain social acceptance at home or outside; divorce, desertion, or death of a parent; parental favoritism toward a sibling; sibling rivalry; strained relationships between stepparent and stepchild; strained relationships with foster parents; economic difficulties; bad experiences at school; bad experiences as a result of race or ethnic background; moving to a new home; being punished by playmates, classmates, and teachers; or depression of the mother.

The signs and symptoms of depression vary with the child's age. In infancy the child may simply fail to thrive. A mother who becomes depressed withdraws from her child, who, in turn, becomes depressed; the baby will not be able to overcome his depression until the mother overcomes hers. A mother substitute may be required until the mother is able to control her emotions. This situation is a serious one: as many as 50 percent of infants who suffer from failure to thrive (considered to be a medical syndrome) die.[6]

Depression in children is often hidden behind a barrage of other symptoms and complaints. Among schoolchildren depression can result in behavior problems that include temper tantrums, absenteeism from school, extreme fears related to school, and academic failure.[7]

Older children may also show depression through abnormal behavior. Depression may manifest itself in angry outbursts, learning difficulties, problems with sleep, and bed-wetting. Overeating is also a common symptom of depression; a child who has been rejected at school or at home often seeks solace in food, and the resulting weight gain simply brings more rejection and self-blame. Some children who are depressed refuse to eat, resulting in starvation. Some resort to seclusion or hatefulness toward friends and family members. Fortunately, suicidal feelings are rare in children before adolescence.

How can you tell if what your child is feeling is real depression and not just a case of the temporary blues? If he continually displays one or more of the following patterns of behavior he could be seriously depressed.[8]

---

[6] Marshall A. Falk, "Treatment of the Depressed Outpatient," *Post-Graduate Medicine,* 55, no. 3 (March 1974), 68-76.

[7] Julius Segal, "Little Boy, Little Girl Blue," *Family Health,* July 1976, p. 39.

[8] Ibid.

1. Lack of self-confidence, evident in a low opinion of himself and his abilities and loss of interest in future activities. He may suffer feelings of defeat, causing him to withdraw into himself and to spend more time alone.
2. Acting out negative behavior, including hostile behavior, hyperactivity, and behavior that is extremely difficult to control.
3. Physical symptoms, such as a change in eating habits, either overeating or undereating; change in sleeping habits, such as broken sleep, tiredness in the morning, or an escape into sleep by remaining in bed; or repetitive problems, such as stomach aches, that cannot be explained by physical disease.

Antidepressant drugs, sometimes effective in the treatment of adult depression, rarely work for a child; a child needs an adult to spend quality time with him, paying extra attention and demonstrating care. Try some of these positive approaches:[9]

1. Let the child know that everyone feels sad and depressed at one time or another. Explain that these feelings are completely normal and that after they pass the child will feel happy again. Some children are frightened and burdened by the anxiety that the depression is a permanent condition.
2. Help the child find an activity that will bolster his spirits: a hobby, a new and engrossing game, a sight-seeing trip, or anything that will interest and excite him.
3. Encourage the child to admit that he feels sad or dejected. He needs to be as honest as he can about his feelings if he is to overcome them successfully.
4. Find a way for the child to experience success. Figure out something that the child does well, or help him use a special skill or talent. Little triumphs can help him rediscover a lost sense of self-esteem.
5. Get the child out of his routine. Introduce some new foods at lunch, take him to a new restaurant, let him take a few days off from school and go to the mountains. You may want to read him a new book. Any of these will help conquer the blues.
6. Above all, listen sympathetically to anything he has to say—even though it may be hard at times for you.

DEPRESSION IN ADOLESCENTS

Depression in adolescents is usually a reaction to loss, whatever its nature might be, and adolescents experience many losses in their difficult progress from childhood to adulthood.

Probably the most common loss in adolescence is that of self-esteem; an

[9] Ibid.

adolescent's need for self-esteem must be filled primarily by the outside world, and there are many rejections in that outside world.[10] But most teenagers bounce back from peer rejection or rejection by adults, and most thrive with the support of family members and friends. Dangerous depressions, those that last a long time, are not uncommon among teenagers, however, and they require early detection and treatment.[11]

Because adolescence is a time of complex pressures it is difficult to determine when an adolescent is depressed; the normal course of events in adolescence results in natural highs and lows of moods. A depressed adolescent will have several different kinds of behaviors: extended apathy (the "I-don't-care" attitude), wide extremes in eating or sleeping habits, withdrawal from peers, rebellion, running away, defiance, aggression, hostility, use of narcotic drugs, compulsive eating, chain smoking, addiction to television, or alcoholism.[12] If the adolescent has a chronic illness—such as diabetes, kidney disease, or tuberculosis—or if the adolescent's parents have marital problems he is especially prone to serious depression. Unfortunately, the first sign of serious depression in an adolescent may be suicide or attempted suicide—a solution the adolescent seeks when all other tries at relief fail him.

The best way to help a depressed adolescent is to show concerned, non-judgmental interest in the teenager and to show by words and actions that you are interested in him, in his problems, and in his happiness—now and in the future. Such treatment goes a long way in helping him overcome feelings of rejection and establishes a relationship he can turn to in times of loneliness.

POSTNATAL DEPRESSION

Our society glorifies motherhood; we are taught that it is wonderful to be pregnant and that the experience of becoming a mother is fraught with nothing but joy and satisfaction. More and more people in our country are getting married and at an earlier age; many women are giving birth to children as a means to fulfill the marriage relationship.

Because of these favorable social attitudes a woman expects to feel marvelous after giving birth to a baby. Most women anxiously await the birth, making eager preparations for what they believe to be a very happy time. A pregnant woman's own mother tells her that nothing in the universe equals the joy she will feel when she holds her newborn child in her arms; her friends watch her

---

[10]Ghislaine D. Godenne, "The Masked Signs of Adolescent Depression," *Medical Insight,* March 1974, p. 9.

[11] Ibid.

[12] Ibid.

thrive during pregnancy, despite its occasional hardships, and listen to her eager anticipations.

For many women all of those feelings are realized; for others, the grief and confusion of postnatal depression become a reality.[13] They feel miserable and unhappy; they experience a letdown, and some even feel like the whole world has fallen down on top of them. They worry about things that aren't worth worrying about; they burst into tears for no reason at all. Instead of feeling joyful and excited when they look at the baby, they feel frustration. Holding the baby creates tension; feeding the baby and changing his diaper are unpleasant. And, to compound the problem, the mother feels guilty about not feeling happy.

This condition is called *postnatal depression* and doctors are unsure about how many mothers are affected by it each year. There are two different times, and two different degrees of severity, for this kind of depression.

The first is immediately after giving birth. While there seems to be no correlation between the amount and severity of the labor itself and the postnatal depression, indications exist that the fatigue caused by labor may contribute to the onset of postnatal depression. Women who suffer depression at this point are not interested in the child and generally don't want anything to do with it. Some mothers resent the child; other mothers may even blame the father. But the kind of depression occurring at this stage passes quickly, and generally by the time the mother is ready to leave the hospital and take the baby home she can scarcely remember a time when she did not cherish the infant.

The second kind of postnatal depression develops at a different time and is much more serious. Once the mother gets the baby home she becomes hysterical and violent. She totally rejects the child; she not only refuses to cradle and cuddle him but may even refuse to stay in the same room with him. A woman suffering this kind of depression is dangerous to herself and to her child. She shows absolutely no concern for the child—if the depression becomes severe enough, she may try to kill the baby—and she may become suicidal. There seems to be no immediate care for this reaction. First steps consist of sedation until the mother reaches a state of calm, after which more involved therapy must be initiated. Luckily, the majority of postnatal depression cases consist of the milder, nonviolent kind that immediately follows birth; few mothers reach the violent stage in which they present a danger to themselves and their infants.

Some mothers suffer a depression after they leave the hospital, but the depression is not violent nor does it pose a particular danger. It is easy to determine the causes for this kind of postnatal depression. When the mother was in the hospital she had help with the infant. She may have been allowed to

[13] David Cohen, "What Is Post-Natal Depression?" *Man & Woman,* vol. 16 (London: Marshall Cavendish, Ltd, 1977), p. 1190.

bathe, feed, and change the baby, but she was not ultimately responsible for the baby's health and survival. Help was always available for the baby, who, of course, is completely dependent on others for life.

But once the mother gets home she is often solely responsible for the child. The baby requires a great deal of attention and hard work. If the baby screams or if the mother is too tired to cope with the demands she can't simply ring for a nurse to take over child care duties. And there are other problems—now that she's back home she's responsible not only for the care of the new baby, but for the care and feeding of her husband, other children she may have, and the upkeep of household responsibilities: laundry, cooking, cleaning. Sometimes it's just too much for her.

In some instances there's still another pressure. The husband's attitude may change; after the birth of a baby the relationship between two marriage partners is not the same. It's never just "the two of us" again; some husbands may come to the sudden realization that they no longer command the complete attention of their wives. A woman with a new baby must of necessity spend a great deal of time with the baby, attending to its physical needs. A husband who is used to being the center of his wife's world may not be able to adjust well to what he perceives as "second place," a reaction that certainly places additional stress on the woman.

There are other reasons for the depression: the readjustment of the body following birth, the changing level of hormones, the anxiety over being a good mother, concern over the changing relationship of husband and wife, the fatigue of constant child care, the alteration of sexual activity for some time following birth.

Postnatal depression, luckily, can be dealt with and can be overcome with a good program of therapy and concern on the part of those who are with the mother. Some suggestions for overcoming the depression include the following.[14]

1. Before birth get advice about parenthood. Simply getting advice and information about being a good parent can help to relieve some of the anxieties you are about to face in becoming a parent. You can ask your own doctor or clinic where to get information or contact a chapter of the International Childbirth Association.

2. Surround yourself with those who have been through the childbirth experience and who can offer you support and help. Make friends with other young couples who have toddlers, and ask them for advice and help. If you plan to breastfeed talk to other mothers who are successfully and happily nursing their own children. You might consider joining the La Leche League for support and information.

[14]Michael Newton, "New Baby! Why So Sad?" *Family Health/Today's Health,* May 1976, pp. 17, 64.

3. Continue pursuing your outside interests, but cut down on the amount of responsibility you accept. If you belong to a club or organization continue to attend meetings and activities; if you have been doing volunteer work arrange to continue it on a part-time basis that will still allow you to care for your child; if you work, you might consider taking a leave of absence, reduction of hours, or freelance options.

4. Arrange for someone to come in and help you with the baby at first. Maybe your husband can rearrange his work schedule or take some vacation so that he can be at home to help you; this might help in several ways by letting your husband feel involved in the care of the baby and by giving the two of you more time together. If your husband is unable to arrange for this kind of a release from work arrange for a close relative, good friend, or nurse to stay at the house with you and help you until you are confident and rested.

5. Don't plan to move just before or just after the baby is born. The birth is a big enough event to adjust to; moving, with its physical demands and its emotional adjustment, is an unwise burden to accept at such a time. You should also be in a neighborhood where you are acquainted with the neighbors so that you will have people you can call on for help.

6. Arrange to attend child care classes at your local hospital; you will learn about labor and delivery and about how to care for your baby after you get home.

7. Make sure that your diet is adequate and especially that it is rich in iron and protein. If you eat properly you will be able to resist the fatigue that so often prolongs and worsens depression.

8. Get plenty of exercise.

9. Even after the baby is born arrange to spend one evening a week away from the house with your husband, kind of a "date." Spend the time together and express your love and concern for each other while you leave the baby with a trusted relative.

10. Take the opportunity to get away from the house periodically so that the stress and pressure of the home do not seem constant. This doesn't have to be a big outing—a trip to the hairdresser, the grocery store, or a friend's house for a brief visit will serve the purpose.

11. Approach any problems openly and honestly. If you coop your feelings up inside you will only end up hurting yourself. If you have doubts about your ability to care for your child talk to your doctor; he can help arrange for a class or a nurse to get you through the difficult period. If you are unsure that your husband really wanted the baby ask him. You can avoid a lot of grief by confronting your feelings and taking care of them.

If you know someone who is depressed there are ways you can help. Try some of the following suggestions.[15]

1. Make sure that he is not placed in a situation he can't handle. Depression results in a tremendously low self-esteem, and the last thing a depressed person needs is to experience failure. You might suggest to his employer that his duties be slightly realigned to relieve some of the burden.

2. Suggest that he accompany you on a short vacation. This needn't be extensive, but it should serve the purpose of giving him a change of scenery. Sometimes things look better when one moves away and is able to look at them in a different perspective.

3. Give the person something else to think about. Take him out for lunch, challenge him to a round of golf, or ask him over to help you with some simple household chores. You might ask a woman to accompany you shopping, or a man to help you plant some new shrubs in your front yard.

4. Don't serve alcohol to him.

5. Help him set a regular schedule of activities that fills his day; keep him busy and involved.

6. Teach him something new, a craft or a skill, that is not too difficult for him to master. Then give him an opportunity to practice the new craft or skill by helping him, or having him help you, make something to give away.

7. Get him involved in some kind of physical exercise. You might take him swimming or hiking or get him involved with you on an athletic team of some kind. You might pick him up before work twice a week for a quick game of racquetball.

8. Praise him genuinely for his accomplishments and his efforts. Find nice things to say about him that are honest and sincere.

9. Get him involved in doing things for others. It is amazing how quickly we can forget our own problems when we become interested and involved with someone else's interests or problems. Ask him to accompany you while you take a loaf of homemade bread to someone who is ill; suggest that he bake a meal for a new father and go with him to deliver it.

---

[15] List compiled from "Depression: When the Blues Become Serious," *Changing Times,* March 1978, pp. 37-39; Rosslyn, *Depression, The Thin Edge;* Mary L. Smith, "Depression—You See It, But What Do You Do About It?" *Nursing '78,* September 1978, pp. 43-45; Kathleen Earley, "The Constant Sorrow," *The Sciences,* November 1974, pp. 13-17; and John Cohen, "How to Cope with Depression," *Man & Woman,* vol. 16 (London: Marshall Cavendish Ltd, 1977), p. 1771.

10. Arrange for a night out with old friends.

11. Help him establish realistic goals for himself; make sure they are short-term goals that he has the means to achieve. He will experience a sense of renewed self-esteem from making some kind of progress or achievement.

12. Let the person make his own decisions; if you allow him this privilege he will feel that he is in control of his life and what happens to him. Helplessness is often a cause of depression.

13. Offer support and understanding; a depressed person doesn't need someone to criticize or reject him. Let him know that you accept him and care for him *no matter what.*

You can get help and advice from any of the following agencies:

The American Psychiatric Association
1700 Eighteenth Street, N.W.
Washington, D.C. 20009

The American Psychological Association
Office of Professional Affairs
1200 Seventeenth Street, N.W.
Washington, D.C. 20036

The National Institute of Mental Health
Public Inquiries Branch, Division of
Scientific and Technical Information
5600 Fishers Lane
Rockville, Maryland 20852

The Mental Health Association
1800 Kent Street
Arlington, Virginia 22209

PREVENTION OF DEPRESSION

Little, if anything, has been done in the area of depression prevention. Many psychiatrists feel that those people with a predisposition to develop depression may exhibit specific characteristics; if these characteristics could be identified and validated perhaps special steps could be taken to help these people to develop more fully their mechanisms for dealing with stress before extremely stressful events occurred. The biggest problem seems to be in agreeing on what the characteristics are of those who are prone to depression.

Early diagnosis and effective treatment appear to be the most valuable steps in preventing severe depression.

10

SUICIDE

● Carol walked through the living room where her parents sat watching television and kissed them good-night. They were both mildly surprised. Carol was sixteen, and hadn't shown a great deal of open physical affection toward them for several years. At the door Carol turned and smiled at them; they were both pleased. They were so lucky—luckier than many of their friends, whose children were mixed up with drugs, were in trouble at school, or were runaways. Carol always got good grades in school and was generally well behaved. And she had many friends.

At seven the next morning Carol's mother found the door to Carol's room blocked when she tried to open it and wake Carol up for school. She called out to Carol, but her frantic calls brought no response. Finally, with a burst of strength, she pushed the door partially open. Carol's dead body was crumpled in a heap on the floor, her arms outstretched toward the door. She had taken thirty-two sleeping pills.[1]

[1]Mary Susan Miller, "Teen Suicide," *Ladies' Home Journal,* February 1977, p. 68. Reprinted with permission.

• Ruth, a middle-aged woman, took a large quantity of barbiturate tablets at 4:30 P.M. one Wednesday afternoon and fell asleep on the kitchen floor in front of the refrigerator. She knew that every working day for the last three years her husband had arrived home at exactly 5:00 P.M. and had headed directly to the refrigerator for a beer, so there was a strong possibility that Ruth would be discovered and rescued. But that Wednesday night Ruth's husband was delayed and didn't reach home until a little past 7:30. Ruth was dead.[2]

• Richard, emotionally unstable following a divorce settlement, swallowed a large number of sleeping pills and went to sleep in his car, which was parked in front of his estranged wife's house. He pinned a note to his chest, saying that he fully expected to be found by her when she returned from a date with another man. His plan didn't go exactly as expected, though. A dense fog settled before midnight, and the woman didn't sight the parked car until late the next morning. Richard had died sometime the night before.

• When Edith's husband threatened to divorce her she ingested ant poison in front of him; he rushed her to a hospital where she received emergency treatment for the arsenic poisoning and where she told hospital staff members that she didn't really want to die. Several days later, though, as a result of the poisoning, Edith developed serious kidney failure and died two weeks later from uremia and cerebral hemorrhage.

• Kent had been having marital difficulties off and on for over two years; early in June he made an appointment with a physician for symptoms suggestive of depression. A few days before his scheduled appointment he failed to show up at the office where he had a small engineering business. Later that day his car, parked on the railroad tracks where they crossed a remote roadway, was demolished by a train and Kent was killed in the accident.

• When twenty-year-old Larry arrived home for Christmas vacation his parents were worried. There was a lot to talk about—his C grades, for instance. It wasn't easy to get into Harvard Law School these days. And then there was the problem with his girlfriend. Larry's father didn't mind him having a fling, everyone does now and then, but this girl was kind of wild. Even Larry admitted that. Larry's parents told him it was about time to settle down.

The tensions ran high during most of the vacation, and Larry's parents were worried that nothing they had said would sink in. But their worries dis-

---

[2]This and the next three examples were adapted from Robert E. Litman, Theodore Curphey, Edwin S. Shneidman, Norman L. Farberow, and Norman Tabachnick, "Investigations of Equivocal Suicides," *Journal of the American Medical Association,* 184, no. 12 (June 22, 1963), 927-28. Copyright 1963, American Medical Association.

solved as they waved good-bye to Larry at the airport; he seemed more relaxed. He smiled.

"See you in June," his father called out. His mother sighed with relief. They had managed to overcome a potentially unpleasant situation. They felt sure that Larry's grade point average would improve, and that he would sever relationships with his girlfriend.

The next day Larry was dead. His girlfriend found him hanging from her shower rod.[3]

• Carl Smith, sixty-seven, lived in the center of the city in a fourth-floor walk-up apartment; he had been widowed for a year and a half, and he had been retired for a year. He had a married son and four grandchildren who lived in the suburbs, but he saw them only occasionally. In January Carl was admitted to the hospital with severe heart problems; he stayed in the hospital for six weeks.

Before he was discharged doctors gave Carl specific instructions about his dietary restrictions and about what kind of medication he would need to take. They asked a social worker to find him another apartment—they thought four flights of stairs were too many for a man in his condition—but Carl stubbornly refused to move, saying that he wanted to "wait for the undertaker in familiar surroundings." Doctors also suggested that he stay with his son until his health improved, but Carl waved aside that suggestion too; he didn't want to be a bother to anybody.

Several weeks later Carl was found dead in his bed. Carl didn't hold a gun to his head or plunge a knife into his chest or swallow a whole bottle of pills, but his death was suicide, nonetheless. He had failed to follow his dietary restrictions, had refused to take his medication, and had continued to climb the four flights of stairs to his apartment. He had never returned to see his doctor.[4]

• Sixteen-year-old Peter and his parents had spent a quiet weekend in their large old frame house in the heart of New Haven, Connecticut. They ate dinner together at a local restaurant on Sunday night and returned to the house, where Peter went to his room to finish his homework while his parents watched television downstairs. About ten o'clock Peter entered the living room and attacked his father from behind with a two-foot ax; the man was dead after several blows. Peter caught his mother as she attempted to run from the room, and he killed her with the ax, too.

A few minutes later Peter walked several blocks to a high-rise apartment building where a friend of his lived. The doorman recognized Peter and joked with him as the boy walked through the lobby and boarded the elevator. Peter

[3]Miller, "Teen Suicide," p. 68.

[4]Margaret O'Keefe Diran, "You Can Prevent Suicide," *Nursing '76,* January 1976, pp. 61-62.

took the elevator to the top floor, climbed a flight of stairs to the roof, and leaped to his own death.[5]

• John was generally described as a cheerful, giving, independent, and solid kind of guy—the "salt of the earth." At the age of sixty-five he was an active person with many hobbies: he loved gardening and maintained an elaborate garden. He was also a sportsman and had enjoyed hunting and golf for a number of years, although his wife's chronic illness had limited his hunting trips for some time.

John and his wife lived moderately within their means; John had apparently planned well and adequately for his retirement, and there had never been any financial stress in their marriage. He was active in the Masonic Lodge and spent hours coaching new initiates on the ritual. Although he had had some difficulty with his eyesight and his wife had suffered with shingles, both were in good health and enjoyed sound physical condition.

One Sunday morning John returned from playing golf with some friends at about 11:30. He joined his wife in the garden, where they spent several hours arranging a detailed bouquet; at about 1:00 they enjoyed lunch at a drive-in restaurant, and afterward they returned to their gardening.

At about 4:00 that afternoon two of John's friends stopped by for a visit; the three enjoyed a drink together and talked about the Masonic Lodge charity event. John expressed excitement that he had sold his quota of tickets to the charity.

When his friends left at about 5:30 John headed for the rumpus room while his wife prepared dinner. While she was fixing the meal she heard something that sounded like a car backfire, but she didn't pay any real attention to the sound. She placed the meal on the table and called John for dinner. There was no response. She went outside to the garden, but John wasn't there; she searched through the rest of the house, finally looking in the bedroom.

John was slumped back on the bed, and a bullet hole was in almost the center of his forehead; there was powder burns around the wound. The bullet had gone almost horizontally from front to back; the gun, a .38 caliber Smith & Wesson revolver, had been one of John's favorite hunting guns; it was lying in his lap.[6]

Suicide—a deliberate act of self-destruction—has fascinated and frightened men from the beginning of time. And it is a major human problem; over 34,000

[5] Francine Klagsbrun, *Youth and Suicide* (New York: Pocket Books, 1976), p. 50. From *Too Young to Die* by Francine Klagsbrun. Copyright © by Francine Klagsbrun. Reprinted by permission of Houghton Mifflin Company.

[6] Paul W. Pretzel, et al., "Psychological Autopsy," *Bulletin of Suicidology*, Fall, 1970, pp. 3-4.

people kill themselves each year in the United States alone. Sadly, that number may be a gross underestimation, since many suicides go unreported or become covered up or disguised. The figure may be closer to 100,000. Even more shocking is the fact that there are more than 5 million attempts to commit suicide each year.[7]

Suicide is in the top ten causes of death in the United States. In the fifteen- to nineteen-year-old group suicide is surpassed as a cause of death only by cancer and accidents. On some college campuses *it is the leading cause of death!*

Suicide is not limited to any one age or social group. People of all ages and colors kill themselves; members of all professions and occupations commit suicide. In some cases the victims seem depressed, hostile, withdrawn; those around them aren't surprised at the news of self-destruction. Other times the victims of suicide seem popular, happy, well adjusted, and at ease with themselves; their act of self-destruction comes as a shock, and acquaintances often deny the obvious, claiming a homicide or illness as the cause of death. In general, there is no certain "type" of person who commits suicide—suicide happens to "nice" people in "typical" families.[8]

But in almost all cases there are "cries for help," even though in some cases the cries may be weak, almost inaudible. Sometimes, in retrospect, survivors are able to recognize these cries for help, yet many were unable to hear the cries in time to save the victim from himself.

You can play an active role in the prevention of suicide by learning to recognize such cries for help and by knowing how to respond to them in the most effective way. The psychological Band-Aid that you help apply may mean the literal difference between life and death for your child, your mate, your colleague, or your friend.

Probably most common are suicides among two distinct age groups: adolescents and the elderly. You can learn to recognize their peculiar characteristics and can act to prevent them.

SUICIDE AMONG ADOLESCENTS

Adolescence is a time of stress, even under the best of conditions. An adolescent is trying to make the difficult transition from childhood to adulthood, and he is plagued by further stresses: drug and alcohol abuse, intense competition (especially academic), and overpopulation (too many people want too many things).

Over 90 percent of the adolescents who attempt suicide feel that their families do not understand them; most feel unappreciated and unloved by their

---

[7]Jan Fawcett, *Before It's Too Late* (West Point, Pa.: Merck Sharp and Dohme, 1979), p. 2.

[8]Ibid.

family members. Those who do attempt to express their feelings of unhappiness or frustration to their parents feel rejected and misunderstood. Most report that they are ignored or that their feelings are denied by others in the family.

Most of those who attempt suicide come from families that stress success and competition, the ability to win. Adolescents who are victims of impossibly high expectations choose to face death rather than face the failure and rejection that will result if they don't "measure up."

In many adolescent suicides there is disorganization of the basic family structure: a broken home, where one of the parents has died or has left due to divorce. The adolescent, then, feels isolation and loneliness and eventually convinces himself that he is unloved.

The adolescent's life may be further complicated by the fact that he has no role models to help him develop his values; he may lack consistent positive reinforcement. He may have poor self-control; he may not be able to solve problems easily. And he may be easily led and influenced by others.[9]

All of these factors combine to give the adolescent a nagging lack of optimism, a lack of hope about the future. As a result the adolescent feels he has no power to turn his life around.

Whatever the reason for self-destruction a suicide rarely occurs without warning. The warning might come in the form of verbal cues—"I'm going to kill myself," "You won't have to worry about me anymore," "Life isn't worth living," or "That won't matter where I'm going"—or the warning might come in the form of behavioral changes. Behavioral changes you should be on the alert for include the following.[10]

1. A dramatic shift in the quality of school performance.
2. Changes in social behavior.
3. Excessive use of drugs or alcohol.
4. Changes in daily behavior and living patterns.
5. Extreme fatigue.
6. Boredom.
7. Decreased appetite.
8. Preoccupation and inability to concentrate.
9. Overt signs of mental illness, such as hallucinations, delusions, talking to oneself.
10. Giving away treasured possessions.
11. Truancy.
12. Failure to communicate with family members and school personnel. Adolescents who reach despair serious enough to lead to suicide often

[9]"Point of No Return: Teenagers and Suicide," *Current Lifestyles,* March 1979, pp. 8-10.

[10]Susan A. Winickoff and H.L.P. Resnik, "Student Suicide," *Today's Education, NEA Journal,* April 1972, p. 32. Used by permission of *Today's Education* and the authors.

choose to talk to a peer or to some other interested individual outside of his family or school associations.

13. Isolation and morose behavior.

14. Insomnia.

15. Lack of a sufficient father-son relationship. This may have occurred either because the father is absent as a result of death or divorce or because the father has been so wrapped up in his career that he has not taken time to develop a relationship with his son.

16. Difficult mother-daughter relationship, especially in the absence of a strong father figure.

17. Pregnancy.

18. Excessive smoking, indicative of tension.

19. A history of child abuse in the home. Early experiences of being battered as a child can spur violence later in adolescence; such violence is usually aimed at the self, resulting in suicide.

20. Apparent "accidental" self-poisoning, especially if the behavior is repeated.

Obviously, any one of these symptoms, or even a combination of them, could be present in the life of a very normal teenager who is *not* contemplating suicide. But whatever you do, don't ignore them. Confront the teenager. Say something like, "I've noticed that you've really lost your appetite lately. Is something bothering you?" Sometimes you won't be able to get the teenager to respond to such a direct approach. Instead, you might try something like, "Do you ever just wish you didn't have to wake up in the morning? Do you ever wish you were dead?" If he says yes you can ask him, "Have you been thinking about killing yourself?"

Don't worry—the suggestion won't inspire someone who hasn't contemplated the act to suddenly plan a suicide. Your purpose is to get the problem out in the open. Because an adolescent who is suicidal is often at a critical point of despair and noncommunication, you will need to take the initiative. Be aggressive. There's a life at stake.

There are some factors about adolescent suicide that you should understand. Some of these factors also apply to suicides among other age groups.[11]

1. A person who talks about suicide is probably serious about committing suicide. Not everybody who commits suicide talks about it first, and not everybody who makes verbal threats follows through, but over 80 percent of those who commit suicide communicate their intentions first. This might be a direct statement—such as "Life isn't worth living anymore" or "I'm going to kill myself"—or it might be extremely subtle—"Want to go for one last ride?" Someone who talks about committing suicide might be asking for help.

[11] Donald E. Berg, "A Plan for Preventing Student Suicide," *School Health Review,* 8 (1969), 206-11. Reprinted by permission of the American Alliance for Health, Physical Education, Recreation and Dance, 1900 Association Drive, Reston, Va. 22091.

Always take a person who talks about suicide seriously. Never treat him lightly or dismiss him. He feels hopeless; by communicating his desires to you, though, he has entrusted you and asked you for your help.

2. The suicide will usually not occur without warning. Be alert for any signs of mental distress, depression, or isolation. Assess the adolescent using the twenty clues listed (pages 123-24); they are all warnings of a serious problem.

3. Actual suicide and attempted suicide are not in the same class of behavior. Of ten adolescents who attempt suicide only one will go on to complete the suicidal act. Girls will attempt suicide eight to nine times as often as their male peers, although the boys will complete the act three times as often. Such attempts are often only a way of getting attention; but such attempts can't be brushed off or the person will eventually, even if accidentally, complete the suicide as he becomes more and more intense in his efforts to gain attention.

4. Economic conditions do not affect suicide among teenages. Adolescents from poor families do not commit suicide any more often than do adolescents from rich families; young people who come from families who are constantly moving under stress *do* commit suicide, but the suicide is a result of isolation, *not* poverty.

5. Suicide is not a problem only of the mentally ill. It is true that adolescents who have mental illness are at a higher risk of committing suicide, especially if they hear voices commanding them to destroy themselves, but suicide can be committed by those who do not suffer from any mental illness at all.

6. Suicide in a family often leads to suicide of a child or adolescent. Suicide is *not* an inherited biological tendency, however; it may be a learned behavior, but it is not genetically transferred from one generation to another.

7. People who attempt suicide are not always intent on dying. They *are* intent on changing something: the way people react to them, the level of self-esteem they enjoy, the intensity of a relationship. Many wish simply to escape from an intolerable situation and would be happy to go on living if they could be removed from that particular situation. Even as they decide to kill themselves most hope for rescue.

8. People can change. Just because a person has attempted suicide once does not mean that he will be suicidal forever. Thoughts about suicide come and go, even among the most healthy individuals.

How can you decide exactly what the risk is?

Unfortunately, there's no sure way, but there are some things that help us determine exactly how serious a person is. First of all, assess the adolescent and determine whether he has exhibited any of the above-cited characteristics. Once you have approached the adolescent and confirmed that he has considered suicide you can determine his seriousness in a couple of ways.

1. How does he plan on killing himself? An adolescent who plans on using a gun is probably very serious—there is little time for intervention or rescue from a gunshot wound. Hanging is another highly lethal method. Ingestion of barbiturates may be a highly lethal method, depending on how well thought out the plan is. About 70 percent of all adolescent suicides are carried out by gunshot and barbiturates. On the other hand, a person who is planning on cutting his wrists probably hopes for rescue.

2. Ask about the plan. Does the teenager have a specific plan with well-worked-out details and timing? If so, he's a high risk. Contrary to popular belief, most suicidal persons will openly discuss a plan for suicide if you ask them about it. On the other hand, a person whose "plan" is vague and not really structured or thought out is probably not as serious.

3. Has the person attempted suicide before? If so, he's an extremely high risk. Of special concern are those who nearly died as a result of a previous suicide attempt.

Never ignore *any* threat of suicide. All of them are to be taken seriously and are to be acted on; simply use this checklist to determine the urgency of the situation.

You can do specific things to help an adolescent who is suicidal.[12]

1. *Listen.* Really listen. Try to really hear what the adolescent is trying to say. Make every possible effort to understand fully what the teenager is trying to say—repeat back to him, in your own words, what he has just said. If you haven't gotten it right, he'll correct you.

2. *Evaluate the seriousness of the situation.* Again, if the teenager has formulated a specific plan, he is probably more serious than the person who is rather vague about his method.

3. *Evaluate the intensity of the emotional disturbance.* A person who has been depressed and then becomes agitated and restless is usually a cause for alarm. Keep in mind that a person may be extremely upset, but not necessarily suicidal.

4. *Take everything the adolescent says seriously.* Never dismiss what the teenager says or disvalue what he says in any way. He might be talking in a low-

---

[12]Calvin J. Frederick, "Self-Destructive Behavior among Adolescents," reprinted with permission from *Keynote* (now called *Connections,* the quarterly magazine of Boys Club of America), vol. IV, no. 3 (May 1976), 3-50.

key manner, but beneath his seemingly calm exterior may be a seething emotional disturbance.

5. *Ask directly whether he has entertained thoughts of suicide.*   You won't plant any seeds. Most of the time a person who *has* contemplated suicide will be relieved at the opportunity to discuss his feelings and will welcome the exchange.

6. *Don't be fooled if the adolescent says the crisis is past.*   A teenager will often feel an initial sense of relief after he has been able to talk to you about his suicidal feelings, but the same thoughts will probably recur later. Followup is critical.

7. *Be affirmative but supportive.*   A person who is distressed needs strong, stable guideposts. Give the impression that you know what you are doing; let the adolescent know that everything will be done to prevent him from taking his life.

8. *Evaluate the available resources.*   Continuing observation and followup are vital to survival. Find out if there is a minister, relative, or friend whom the teenager would feel comfortable with; if there is contact that person and explain the situation. Wait with the adolescent until the other helper arrives. In some communities there are suicide crisis centers that can provide valuable help.

9. *Act specifically.*   Do something tangible. Give the person something to hang on to. Arrange to see him later, and make sure that there is someone else for him to depend on. Nothing is more frustrating for a person in trouble than to feel that he gained nothing from the confrontation.

10. *Ask for assistance and consultation.*   Use your community resources.

Some additional hints will help you in dealing with a suicidal adolescent.

Arrange for someone who is responsible and receptive to stay with the teenager during the acute crisis. Never leave someone who is threatening to kill himself alone; he may panic and complete the self-destruction immediately.

Don't treat the adolescent with horror. Chances are feelings of rejection led to his suicidal thoughts in the first place. The last thing he needs is to be rejected again—this time by a person in whom he placed his trust and confidence. Treat him with respect and kindness.

Never deny the adolescent's suicidal thoughts. They are real to him, no matter how ridiculous they seem to you. Acknowledge them; coax the person to talk about his thoughts and feelings and to express his emotions. Sometimes he's confused more than anything else; just talking about it will help.

Make sure that the adolescent's environment is safe and free of provocation. Someone who is desperate enough to consider self-destruction should not be teased and tantalized with the sight of a handgun, a bottle of sleeping pills, a sharp knife, or a convenient place to hang himself by his belt.

Never challenge an adolescent in an attempt to shock him out of his ideas. The story is told of the high school student who crawled out on the ledge of a high building on campus, threatening to jump. A crowd gathered on the ground below; a middle-aged teacher, hoping to shock the boy back into reality, cajoled, "Go ahead! Jump!" The teenager plunged to his death at the invitation of the teacher.

Don't try to win arguments about suicide. They simply cannot be won. A person who has decided on suicide as a viable alternative has usually undergone a long process of considering and eliminating various other methods of solving his problem. He's convinced that suicide is the only way out, and he's convinced that he's right. Instead of getting into an argument concentrate on winning his confidence and trust.

Tell the adolescent that his feelings of depression are temporary and will pass. Do not try to lessen the severity of his feelings in any way; instead, identify with them, certify that they are real, and tell him of some incident of your own experience when you felt particularly bleak and depressed. Help him to realize that, no matter how bad things look now, he *will* start to feel better if he gives himself the chance.

Help the adolescent realize that if he chooses to die the choice is permanent and the decision can never be reversed. Help him understand that if he chooses some other way of coping with his problem—hospitalization, counseling, a move to another town—he can always change his mind and try something else. But if he chooses to die he will not be free to change his mind later and choose something else instead. Point out that, while he is alive, the adolescent can always get help and possibly resolve his problems. Point out also that death is final. There can be no chance for resolution of problems after death. In all of his upset, this is something he probably has not stopped to consider.

Make the adolescent realize what he will do to the survivors. Of course, this would not be a good point to focus on if you have been able to determine that the motive for suicide is somehow to punish someone the adolescent is close to, particularly his parents. Talk about the tremendous guilt and pain that will remain with his parents and siblings; make him realize how much his friends will suffer. Explain the terrible stigma that is attached to suicide. If he dies he will be free from the pain and the stigma, but those he leaves behind will suffer for the rest of their lives.

If you can determine that the motivation for suicide is not related to the desire to punish or get even with family members, call family members in to help establish a lifeline with the adolescent. They need to express their love for him and their support of him. From talking to the adolescent you have probably been able to determine *why* he wants to kill himself. If you can, talk privately with the parents and other family members about the motive; if they have been pressuring him too heavily in school ask them to mention some areas where he has done good work and praise him for them. Ask them to also confront the issue of their pressuring him; perhaps a meaningful dialogue between them can start to relieve the pressures that have built up.

Above all, allow the teenager to ventilate his feelings. The fact that he has held his feelings in for a long time has brought him to the point of suicide. He needs to explode—to honestly confront the thoughts he's having. Encourage him to be verbal and expressive, even if others are there—especially his parents, since a lot of his problems have probably stemmed from his relationship with them. Let him know that the situation will be less threatening because you, and possibly others, are there; he's not alone with his parents, so he doesn't need to be fearful of being open and honest.

Never leave a suicidal adolescent alone, isolated, or unobserved for any appreciable length of time.

In all your dealings with a suicidal adolescent do everything possible to preserve his dignity, self-worth, and sense of personal value. Build him up, and perhaps he will overcome the need to tear himself down.

SUICIDE AMONG THE ELDERLY

The group most vulnerable to suicide in the whole age spectrum is the elderly.[13] In fact, the rate of accomplished suicide among older white males is higher than that for any other age, sex, and race combination; older white males accomplish self-destruction five times more often than the entire population and twelve times more often than elderly females. Almost one-fourth of all suicides reported annually are people over the age of sixty-five.

Why?

Aged suicidal persons are often sad, tired, and lonely. These factors combine to produce deep depression. In some elderly people depression is obvious; others manage to mask their feelings of depression, but the very process of hiding such disturbing feelings often leads to self-violence.

Another major factor is physical illness. In fact, serious physical disease can be a major factor in influencing a decision to commit suicide.

How can you tell that an elderly person has become suicidal?

Evaluate all of the person's life events. Is he depressed? Is he ill? Especially take note of whether he has an illness from which he believes he will never recover. Is there a possibility that he could be suffering from some kind of a mental disorder? How are his finances? Does he have enough money to sustain himself, or does he appear to be seriously denying himself things that he needs? Has he been forced to surrender his independence by moving in with you, another child, a friend, or an extended care facility? Has he lost his mate? Are

---

[13] David Rachlis, "Suicide and Loss Adjustment in the Aging," *Bulletin of Suicidology,* Fall 1970, pp. 7-9.

his children far away, or does he have no children? What is he like as a person? Has he been able throughout his life to adjust easily to frustration? Is he a resourceful person?

By asking yourself all of the above questions you can build for yourself a basis of understanding *why* the elderly person might feel that self-destruction is the best possible alternative. Of course, there are several obvious behavioral cues; always be suspicious in the case of severe depression or severe mental disorientation.

An elderly person will usually give you some indication of his intent to kill himself, as will suicide victims of any age. Remember, that indication of intent may not always be verbal. Of course, sometimes he will say something obvious ("I think I'd be better off dead") or something more subtle ("You would be happier if I were out of the way"), but often the cues will be nonverbal. He may suddenly become obsessed with making up a will. Or he may suddenly begin to dispose of property. Take note of the person who begins methodically cleaning out drawers, closets, and cupboards; watch the person who starts giving away things he has treasured all his life to favorite grandchildren or neighbors.

A special risk is a person who has been depressed for a long period of time and who suddenly becomes very cheerful. High risk is also indicated by elderly people who express guilt or grief over becoming a burden or "being in the way."

One of the most widely used suicide prevention techniques for elderly victims is a therapeutic program of antidepressant drugs; in some cases physicians use the antidepressant drugs along with medication that acts as a muscle relaxant. In some severe cases electroshock therapy may be needed.[14] In many cases doctors like to treat the elderly in a hospital for a brief length of time so they can judge reaction to the drugs and the patient's general state of mind, and so they can detect any physical problems that may be partially responsible for the depression.

You should make certain that any elderly person who seems to be unusually depressed see a doctor; if the person is also ill you will probably need to arrange transportation and possibly accompany the person to the doctor. Some elderly people may resist seeing a doctor for financial reasons; try to find a way to help out without reducing the person's self-esteem or independence.

Once an elderly person has been treated by a physician there is much his family can do to help discourage suicidal feelings. Help the person be more useful; if he is living in your home give him definite tasks to do and let him, and other family members, know that he is solely responsible for those tasks. Build his self-esteem; if there was something that he particularly enjoyed when he was younger, or something he did particularly well, let him do it now. For instance, if his hobby was gardening turn over a section of your garden to him, and give

---

[14] Robert L. Garrard, "Is Your Elderly Patient Talking about Suicide?" *Consultant,* January 1973, p. 50.

him free reign. Praise his efforts. Display a floral arrangement from his garden at dinner some Sunday, and express appreciation for the beauty he brings into your home. Make sure that the tasks and assignments you give him do not jeopardize his health, and make sure that he has the physical and mental capacity to complete the tasks. The doctor can help you know what he can and cannot do. If you assign him some task that he cannot complete because of physical restrictions, he will simply end up feeling failure and frustration.

Show the elderly person that you appreciate his situation. Let him talk about it if he wants to; genuinely listen. He probably has frustrations he'd like to talk over with someone who'd listen.

Include the elderly person in your family activities, or, if necessary, plan some activity just for him. Make sure that his needs and requirements are taken into consideration when you plan family outings or activities that include him.

Pay special and appropriate attention to his general health. Remember, many suicides among the elderly occur because people are afraid to deal with chronic illness. Make the person as comfortable as you can, and make sure that he has adequate medication and other requirements that will help him through this difficult period of poor health. Encourage him to follow his doctor's recommendations, and make his health care routine as pleasant as possible. For instance, if the doctor recommends that he take a short walk every afternoon, try to see that someone from the family accompanies him each time. Pleasant conversation and a chance to be with someone can lighten the burden considerably.

Above all, try to alleviate his loneliness. Spend time with him, and suggest that others also do so. To inspire an elderly person to want to keep on living you must show him that there is satisfaction and joy to be gained from life.

SUICIDE PREVENTION

What can you do to help someone who may be contemplating suicide?

The first, and most obvious, thing you can do is to be alert. Learn what the clues are. Notice when someone you know issues strong verbal or behavioral clues. Listen to a person's cries for help.

The saddest, and most common, phrase heard by someone who deals with suicide is, "I didn't think he'd really do it." A close follow-up is, "He just wasn't the type." Suicide can happen to anyone; and anyone who says he is going to do it should be taken at his word.

There is a cardinal rule in suicide prevention: *Do something. Get help.* Find out all you can, and give the person something to hang on to. A suicidal person is depressed, disoriented, confused, and sometimes angry. He usually feels hopeless. You need to offer hope.

Confront the person and talk freely to him. Ask him general and specific questions about his plans to commit suicide. Don't belittle him, don't dehumanize him in any way. Let him know that you understand what he is feeling; never deny him the feelings he is having. And most important, never react with horror or revulsion—a suicidal person has probably already experienced rejection (in fact, it's probably contributed to his suicidal feelings); he needs to know that you accept him. Your acceptance will reduce his guilt and increase his feelings of hope.

The person you are dealing with may be torn between the desire to live and the desire to die. You still have a chance to convince him that he should increase his desire to live. You should always remain calm and display gentle interest, concern, and warmth. Always emphasize the person's positive character traits and the beneficial aspects of his environment. Be supportive and affirmative. It always helps to offer advice and alternatives to someone who feels hopeless and helpless. He needs support now; he needs to know that someone cares for him and wants him to stay alive.

Get help. But never leave the person unattended. In a crisis he may act out of panic as soon as you leave to get help. If possible send someone else for help; if not ask the person to come with you to a hospital or crisis center. Or use the telephone in his presence. Whatever you do, explain calmly and kindly to him that you care about him, that you want him to stay alive, and that you are going to get some people who will help him work out his problems.

Talk to the person. Try to determine what is causing him to feel that he has to kill himself. Usually depression is involved; sympathize with the person, and let him know sincerely that you know how awful depression can be. Tell him that you have been depressed at times, too. But tell him that the depression, no matter how bad it is, is temporary; it will go away. One successful therapist tells his patients that they can kill themselves as soon as they aren't depressed— none of them do.

Stress to the person that a decision of suicide is final. Once he makes the choice to die, and once he dies, he can't change his mind. Offer to help him make some other choices, try some other things out that might help him solve his problems. Make him realize that there *are* alternatives, that death is *not* the only solution.

Beware of presumed fast recoveries. This may signal the relief that the person feels when he has made the decision to follow through with his intentions to commit suicide.

At times the suicide may be prompted by serious mental illness, an overdose of drugs, or intoxication, and the person may not be responsive to your efforts. In such a situation it is important that you make sure the person is with someone at all times and that you send for help. If the situation is intense call for an ambulance; if the person will agree to accompany you and does not pose a threat to you or others take him to a hospital or mental health clinic.

Almost all suicide victims desperately need help—help in coping, help in working out problems that seem insurmountable, help in wanting to live. Find out what resources are available in your community; check your local hospital, your mental hospital, and special mental health groups. Find out if there's a crisis line in your community, and find out how to use it. The more resources that are available to the person, the more likely that the crisis can eventually be overcome.[15]

Finally, the most important thing you can do is offer your friendship and your support. Chances are the suicide was prompted in part by feelings of isolation, loneliness, and loss. A suicidal person desperately needs to have the support and care of others. And that support and care is even more important after the suicidal act, when members of his family and others in the community may shun him because of the suicide attempt. He needs people he knows he can trust and depend on to accept him and to love him despite his attempt at self-destruction. He needs to feel worthy of affection, worthwhile as a human being. He needs to have a reason to live and to overcome the problems that prompted the thought of suicide in the first place.

The most valuable gift you can give him is yourself.

---

[15] Corrine Loing Hatton, et al., *Suicide: Assessment and Intervention* (New York: Appleton-Century-Crofts, 1977), p. 33.

11

EMOTIONAL ASPECTS
OF ILLNESS

The man with cancer of the colon, the woman with multiple sclerosis, the child with leukemia, the adolescent crippled for life in an automobile accident—all have critical and, in some cases, terminal physical conditions. Those physical conditions are characterized by pain, by immobility, by numerous medical treatments, and by necessary alterations in life-style. And because the physical characteristics are so vast, they are often accompanied by emotional problems that, if extreme enough, can be more debilitating and devastating than the physical illnesses themselves.

Any person faced with the prospect of major physical illness, of surgery, of imminent death from illness, or of drastic alteration in life-style because of physical illness is susceptible to the emotional trauma that accompanies any change in physical well-being. A vital part of the medical treatment and rehabilitation of such individuals consists of helping them to cope with the illness, of treating the emotional aspects of the illness. This treatment involves the doctors and nurses who help the patient—but it also involves you, the husband, wife, mother, father, brother, sister, or friend.

WHAT YOU CAN DO TO HELP

You are equipped, surprisingly enough, to help someone who is chronically or terminally ill to adjust to his illness and to live as full and rich a life as possible in light of the disease.[1] A high-school sophomore is obviously ill-equipped to administer complicated medications to his best friend, but he can perform other services that are just as vital in maintaining his friend's emotional health.

You might gain confidence from realizing that doctors and other health care professionals are not better equipped to help a terminally or chronically ill person emotionally. In fact, it may be extremely difficult for a medical professional to talk to someone who is seriously ill. The medical professional must realize, with reality, that medicine does not have all the answers—something that's hard to face. This discomfort is twofold; the ill person also wants to trust the doctor as a person who will make him well again.

You, then, are best equipped, and have at your fingertips the techniques that will help a loved one who is seriously ill. Following is a list of things that almost anyone can do to help an ill person enrich his life.

1. Face up to the illness. Acknowledge your own troubled feelings about the illness. Don't breeze merrily in and out of the hospital room or the person's home without mention of the illness. A person who is dying of brain cancer doesn't want to be regarded as if he has a head cold that will clear up next week; he doesn't want everyone to dwell on his illness, but he does want it to be *acknowledged.* Sometimes the most difficult thing for a terminally ill person to do is to accept the fact that he is dying, to leap the hurdle of denial. It hardly seems worth his effort if everyone else seems to be ignoring the whole thing.

2. Try to resolve your own feelings about the illness. You may feel guilty, responsible, sorry, resentful, or ashamed. Confront your own feelings. Work them out. You are *not* responsible for this person's situation—no one is. If you feel resentful because you realize that the person's illness will necessitate a huge sacrifice of your own time and resources and if you are unable to overcome your resentfulness, get someone to come in and help you care for the ill person. Or

---

[1] Dorothy W. Smith, "Survivors of Serious Illness," *American Journal of Nursing*, March 1979, pp. 441-46; Jerome S. Levy and Russell C. Striffler, "When Religious Belief Affects Therapy," *Patient Care*, November 1, 1974, pp. 99-101; Zvi Lothane, "Preparing the Family for Post-Operative At-Home Convalescence," *Practical Psychology for Physicians*, June 1976, pp. 35-37; Harry S. Abram, "The Psychology of Chronic Illness," *Journal of Chronic Disease*, 25 (1972), 659; "Living with Chronic Neurological Disease: An Interview with Irving S. Cooper," *Practical Psychology for Physicians*, April 1976, pp. 50-63; Thomas J. Luparello, "For Some, Illness Pays," *Medical Insight*, February 1974, pp. 12-19; Allen E. Willner and Charles J. Rabiner, "Surgery: Preventing Emotional Complications," *Practical Psychology for Physicians*, June 1976, pp. 21-29; and G.P. Maher-Loughnan, "Emotional Aspects of Chest Diseases," *Geriatrics*, June 1971, pp. 120-39.

hire a housekeeper to clean the house so that you will be free for other things when you aren't required to be with the sick person. It's important for you to work out your own feelings before you can be of help to the other person.

3. If you have questions concerning the diagnosis and prognosis, especially if the patient is a family member, talk with the doctor. Ask questions. Don't finish until you're clear about what is happening, what the disease will do to the person, and what treatments will be tried. Find out how the treatments will be likely to affect the person. A woman whose husband started chemotherapy for bone cancer was shocked and almost hysterical when he began to vomit violently; no one had told her that vomiting was natural with some kinds of chemotherapy. You need to know exactly what is going on so that you can start your own process of acceptance.

4. Try hard to keep things normal. Of course, a terminal or chronic illness will necessitate some changes; you may need to construct a ramp for a wheelchair where your front porch steps are now, for example. But try to keep routines the same as they have always been. The terminally ill person, as well as the other family members, needs to have consistency and normalcy as much as is possible. If you can let him stay in his own room in his own bed, unless, of course, you must rent or buy a hospital bed; even then, keep it in his own room if you can. If he is able to sit up and feed himself let him eat at the table, where he's always eaten. If he can go to school or to church let him go. If your family has a tradition of popcorn and television on Sunday nights keep it up, and include the sick person if you can. If Uncle George comes over once a week for dinner make sure he knows he is still invited. In essence, preserve as much of the person's life-style as you possibly can.

5. Talk about your feelings regularly with the others who are involved. If you are a parent who is caring for a chronically ill child discuss your feelings frequently with other children in the family and with your spouse. Strive to keep things out in the open; it's dangerous when people around the sick person start to repress feelings and fail to be open and honest. The ill person will be able to sense that people aren't being honest with him, and he may begin to blame himself for the problems that are going on around him.

6. Talk often and openly to the ill person if he wants to talk. He's probably got a lot on his mind, and he probably needs a listening ear. When you do talk to him don't criticize his thoughts and emotions; instead, let him know that you understand, or are trying to understand, how he feels. Sit down when you talk to the person—you will communicate better than if you are pacing or standing. Let the person know that the time you spend with him is his. Listening is your best defense against the ill person's fears; devote your time to allaying specific fears. Recognize that the sick person is a unique individual and that he is vulnerable because of his specific circumstances; draw on your own experiences with vulnerable feelings. Realize that many of the person's fears stem from fear of abandonment rather than fear of the disease itself.

7. Peer group association is important to the patient's emotional adjustment. If you're a member of a bowling team or golf foursome stop over to visit after the bowling game or golf tournament. Don't worry; instead of feeling left out and resentful that he can no longer join you, your friend will feel included and important and will decide that he is still a valuable member of your group, even though he can no longer participate on the golf course or at the bowling alley.

8. If the ill person is experiencing a severe restriction in activity help him compensate with other activities that he *can* participate in. A high school basketball player who can no longer attend and participate in the games might be invited to write newspaper articles about the team. He'll still feel involved and valuable.

9. Emphasize things about the person other than his illness. Chances are, the only thing that's being recognized these days is the disease. Instead, get into a discussion about the patient's art abilities or a Lion's Club convention that he recently participated in. Talk about the patient, but talk about other things, unless, of course, the patient *wants* to talk about his disease. Give the patient something to do, and recognize him for his achievement.

10. Make sure that the patient fully understands any treatment that he is to undergo *before* the scheduled treatment date. An adult should have his questions answered honestly and fully; a child, while unable to understand complicated medical jargon, should be told in simple terms that she can understand what is going to happen. Explaining treatment to a patient allays fears and instills a sense of self-worth.

11. If there are several alternative courses of treatment available a doctor should consult with the patient, if he is an adult, or with the parents, if the patient is a child, before making any decision. Ideally, the decision should be a joint one, and, if possible, the patient should take part in it. This gives the patient a sense of control over his fate and a sense of self-respect.

12. Help the patient resolve any stress situations that may have been present before his illness and that remain unresolved. If he was in financial trouble provide him with a way to earn money. Or, if he is debilitated and is extremely worried about the situation loan him the money or arrange for someone else to loan it to him. If a man was having marital difficulties with his wife help him decide on ways to resolve the problems that were causing the difficulties. You may be limited in much of your ability to help, but offer your assistance anyway.

13. If there are medication procedures that can be carried out at home ask to learn them, and then administer medication at home. A woman whose husband was dying of stomach cancer learned to administer medication with a hypo-

dermic needle, and she was able to give her husband his pain medication at home, thus avoiding a hospital stay and frequent trips to the doctor's office. The man's life-style was preserved as much as possible, and the family was not disrupted as much as they could have been.

14. If the patient is taking medication find out what it is and what its side effects are. You may get angry at a child for refusing to eat his dinner unless you understand that his medication also acts to suppress his appetite.

15. Find out exactly what the patient can and can't do. And then let him do as much for himself as he can. If your five-year-old's doctor tells you that playing with the neighbors won't hurt conquer your tendency to be overprotective. Treat him like you did before if you can. Of course, if such playing would place him in danger of his life you should use prudence and caution; your doctor can be your best source of information. If you wife can still eat at the table don't insist on feeding her in bed. Ill people, as well as those who aren't ill, need to feel a sense of accomplishment and achievement. Let them feed and clothe and bathe themselves as long as possible.

16. Don't impose on other family members. It's important for the ill person to feel normal and accepted, but if he has degenerated to the point where he vomits when he eats or where he can't chew his food without dribbling it down his chin, he is obviously not fit to be at the table with the other family members, where he may cause disgust and resentment. At this point it is best for one family member to help the patient eat in his own room and for other family members to spend time with the patient at other periods of the day.

17. Don't seem preoccupied with the patient's illness. He knows it's there, and he may become overly anxious if you seem too concerned. "I must be closer to dying than I had thought, or Dad wouldn't come in here so often, asking me all these questions."

18. Realize that the illness is taxing the patient's emotions. Be patient with hostile outbursts, episodes of crying, or inability to deal with things in general.

19. If the patient is physically disabled as a result of the disease make sure that the house is safe for him. Tack down carpets and rugs, avoid waxing floors to a bright polish, make sure that hallways and stairways are brightly lit, get a nonskid bath mat for the tub, have ramps constructed where there are stairways, and have a walker or cane handy so that he can get out of bed and get up and down on the toilet. Place a bell next to his bed so he can ring if he needs something.

20. Respect the patient's need for privacy. It's demanding for a formerly independent, vibrant person to be so handicapped that all of his personal habits must now become public. If at all possible help an ill person to the bathroom, but then leave him alone for an unhurried private time. This is especially important for colostomy victims, who need some private time every other day to care for their stoma. If you need to give a bed bath keep the patient covered to preserve his modesty; as you finish up, leave the patient with a pan of clean warm water and a bar of soap, and let him cleanse his genitals himself if he possibly can while you busy yourself somewhere else in the house. Even very sick people can brush their own teeth and sit up on the toilet alone; only when the patient's condition becomes critical should you take over for him.

21. If the patient has strong religious beliefs try to arrange for a member of his church ministry to visit. It may bring great comfort to a terminal patient to be able to take the sacrament at home or to hear a condensed version of last Sunday's sermon. Invite the pastor or bishop to your home and arrange for some quiet time for him to be alone with the patient.

22. It may help the patient to be with others who have the same illness or who have other illnesses that are terminal. While such an encounter should not be frightening or morbid it may prove helpful for the patient to learn that he is not alone in what he is feeling, that his feelings and reactions are normal and that they are shared by others.

23. Do anything you can to preserve the patient's sense of community. Encourage her to visit others, to get involved in a volunteer project, or to visit other ill people if her health permits it. If she's been involved with a bridge group make sure she still attends if her health is good enough. There's a stigma attached to illness, and people who are well-informed and sensitive can help conquer this feeling.

24. Be sensitive to the patient's need for beauty. One cancer victim was depressed about the "aesthetic offensiveness" of his own body and became increasingly depressed at the necessity of looking at his spindly arms, his sunken eyes, his thinning hair, his scaly lips. His family moved his bed to a different room with a spectacular view of the mountains—the room happened to be the family dining room, but the family started eating someplace else so the patient could sit by the window. They took him for rides as often as he could tolerate it, driving through the beautiful canyons near their home. A friend brought over a feather hatband he had started, and the patient finished it shortly before his death. The stark white sheets on his hospital bed were replaced with an interesting masculine print in black and brown, and his sister brought brightly colored flowers in to the bedside almost every day. The patient became so surrounded with beauty that he forgot about his own lack of beauty.

25. If the patient is having an extremely difficult time adjusting or coping provide professional help. You may need to get a psychiatrist or counselor to help with the patient; never make the patient feel stupid for needing such help. Accept the psychiatrist or counselor into your home and commend the patient for his efforts at adjustment.

In our concern with the physical well-being of chronically and terminally ill people we often forget that the emotional turmoil that's raging inside can be even more devastating. By taking the time to understand and to preserve the patient's self-respect and self-reliance you can help ease the way for a person who is otherwise faced with only a rocky path ahead.

12

DRUG AND ALCOHOL EMERGENCIES

The abuse of drugs and alcohol has become an increasingly widespread and serious problem in the United States; alcoholism and drug abuse now strike all classes of people and almost every age group. There are 6 to 10 million alcoholics in the United States today; alcohol is directly involved in about thirty thousand deaths and half a million injuries each year in automobile accidents. And because of its effects on the liver, pancreas, central nervous system, and other body organs, alcohol reduces a person's average life span by about ten to twenty years.

A great deal of research has been published that examines the medical aspects of drug and alcohol abuse. These medical aspects are important, but the other aspects of drug and alcohol abuse, the psychological and social ones, are equally serious.

Many factors unique to the drug or alcohol user can affect how the individual will react and in what long-term ways the individual will suffer from the drug use. In general six factors lead to a more severe reaction from drugs or alcohol.[1]

METHOD OF TAKING THE DRUG   A drug that is taken orally enters the bloodstream more slowly and, therefore, takes longer to start acting. Overdoses are less frequent when drugs are taken orally because the user can easily see how much of the drug he's taking. Drugs injected into the bloodstream have a much more immediate impact. Injection can also lead to other complications, including impurities injected into the bloodstream with the drug; the threat of disease, especially hepatitis from dirty needles; allergic reactions where the drug was injected; and accidental damage to the blood veins.

PRESENCE OF OTHER ILLNESS   When the body's immunity is reduced and its systems weakened by the presence of disease such as epilepsy, diabetes, heart disease, and other conditions, the reaction to drugs is more pronounced. In addition, some drugs can trigger medical reactions such as epileptic seizures. In some cases victims of disease or illness can develop a tolerance to drugs taken to control the disease; for instance, a person who suffers from chronic headaches may develop a tolerance to pain relieving medication, requiring more and more to kill the pain.

SUDDEN WITHDRAWAL   Sudden withdrawal usually results from a situation where the user runs out of money and can no longer purchase the drug or the alcohol; serious medical complications and sometimes death can result from these sudden withdrawals. Besides running out of money there are other reasons for sudden withdrawal: a vacationing doctor (hence the inability to obtain a prescription), incarceration in jail, or a physician who suddenly realizes that a patient has been abusing the drug and abruptly cuts off the supply.

ONSET OF TREATMENT   A person who learns that he will be receiving treatment for drug or alcohol abuse may suffer severe reactions from his anxiety and concern over the planned treatment.

[1] National Institute on Drug Abuse, *National Polydrug Collaborative Project Treatment Manual 1: Medical Treatment for Complications of Polydrug Abuse* (Rockville, Md.: National Institute on Drug Abuse with the Public Health Service of the U.S. Department of Health, Education, and Welfare and the Alcohol, Drug Abuse, and Mental Health Administration, 1978), pp. 1-3.

OTHER LIFE TRAUMAS   A person who has lost his job, had a sister die, been rejected by a lover, lost a friend, or had a severe argument with a family member will react more severely to drugs or alcohol. Such traumas may also alter his drug-taking habit. A person who is addicted to one drug may begin taking additional drugs when such traumas occur.

STRESS   Worry over money, disintegrating relationships, or stress on the job can alter a person's mental condition and can make him more susceptible to the effects of drugs and alcohol. When a person is under stress smaller amounts of the drug create the same effect, and, because he is under stress he has a natural tendency to take larger amounts of the drug to begin with.

WHAT YOU CAN DO TO HELP

Dealing with drug and alcohol emergencies is difficult because often you will be unable to tell exactly *which* drug the person has been taking. Some general guidelines apply to all kinds of drug and alcohol emergencies, however, and will be helpful as you attempt to deal with such emergencies.[2]

DO NOT PANIC   Your first impulse will probably be to toss cold water in the person's face or to move the victim around, trying to help him shake off the drug's effects. Squelch these impulses. Of course, you should move a person if he is in danger—if he is in a burning building, or lying on a roadway.

GET MEDICAL HELP QUICKLY   Don't worry about trying to make a diagnosis. Send for medical help, even if you are unsure that the person needs it. Some drugs can lead to serious medical complications, such as increase in blood pressure or seizures, that can result in permanent damage or death. Don't leave the person alone; send someone else to call for help.

SEARCH THE AREA QUICKLY   While you're waiting for medical help to arrive look around the victim and see if you can determine any clues. You might find a pill bottle, an alcohol bottle, pills, syringes, or other drug equip-

---

[2] Information adapted from Ottawa, Can.: The Minister of National Health and Welfare, *Bad Trips, Freakouts, and Overdoses,* 1975, pp. 8-9; Helen I. Green and Michael H. Levy, *Drug Misuse . . . and Human Abuse* (New York: Marcel Dekker, Inc., 1977), pp. 83-85, 472-74, 497-98; H.L.P. Resnik, Harvey L. Ruben, and Diane Daskal Ruben, eds., *Emergency Psychiatric Care* (Bowie, Md.: Charles Press Publishers, Inc., 1975), pp. 83-85; Patti Lowery and John Schulz, *Diagnosis and Evaluation of the Drug Abusing Patient* (Rosslyn, Va.: National Drug Abuse Center, November 1976), p. 3; and *Emergency Treatment of the Drug Abusing Patient* (Rosslyn, Va.: National Drug Abuse Center, 1978), 1, no. 4, 5-9.

ment. If there are friends or family members around who might know what happened ask them for information.

DON'T ACCUSE OR CRITICIZE THE VICTIM   Be quiet, calm, and gentle with a person who is conscious; help him realize what is happening, and help him realize that what he feels is because of the drug and that it *will* go away. A person who is panicked over his strange mental condition needs reassurance that a drug, and not mental illness, has caused it.

NEVER LEAVE THE PERSON ALONE   No matter what the circumstances, never leave an intoxicated or drugged person alone.

PROVIDE REALITY   Remind the person who you are, and use his name when you address him. Explain thoroughly that you are there to help him. If the person is responsive help provide reality by asking the person to identify the familiar things around him: his favorite chair, a television program, a newspaper, or family members.

ANTICIPATE CONCERNS   As you work with the person try to anticipate the concerns that he will have and the concerns that his family members will have. Plan ahead what you can do to calm these worries.

MAINTAIN EYE CONTACT   Touch the person if it is appropriate; a touch can be reassuring if the person is not hostile or aggressive. Keep your own posture relaxed as you work with the person; if you tense up he will sense that you are anxious and afraid.

ENCOURAGE THE PERSON TO TALK TO YOU   Talk directly to the person; don't communicate to him through others. Ask him clear, simple questions that can be understood by him even in his muddled condition; ask your questions one at a time and slowly. If the person is having trouble thinking or speaking ask questions that require only a simple "yes" or "no." Remember that the person will probably repeat the same things over and over again; don't become impatient.

HELP THE PERSON GAIN CONFIDENCE IN YOU   Listen carefully, without judging him, to what the person has to say. Respond to his feelings; let him know that you understand how he feels and that you are not critical. If the person starts to make progress acknowledge it and tell him you are pleased.

HANDLING A HOSTILE PERSON

You need to take certain precautions if the drug or alcohol victim is hostile or aggressive.

1. If you can, take the person to the hospital immediately. If at all possible keep something familiar with the person: a family member, a friend, a coat, or some other possession.

2. Let the person sit near the door of the room; don't place any obstacle (person or furniture) between the person and the door. In other words don't block his route of escape. A person who feels that he is being trapped in a room and that he has no chance of escape will likely become more anxious, which will exaggerate his hostility and violence.

3. Never approach a potentially violent person by yourself. Quickly estimate how many people it would take to contain the person *completely,* and approach the person in the company of that many people. If you merely attempt to restrain the person and fail he will become more hostile and violent. It's better to wait for help and do nothing than to risk being injured.

4. If you sense that the person is losing control do anything you have to to avoid getting hurt. Watch for a person who seems agitated, who is sweating excessively, or who is talking rapidly while struggling to contain his violent impulses. Leave the room, call in other people to help, or turn the person over to others. If you have to, run to get out of the room.

5. If the person is armed call the police. You should also call the police if the person is unarmed but you cannot find enough people to completely restrain him. In these cases stay away from the person entirely.

MEDICAL DANGER SIGNS

While it is always wise to call for medical help in cases of drug or alcohol abuse six signs signal immediate danger to the person's life. If any of these six signs are present indicate to medical personnel when you call them that the person's life is endangered.

> *Unconsciousness.* The person cannot be awakened; or, if you can awaken him he lapses back into unconsciousness almost immediately. The person may appear to be in a deep sleep or coma.
> *Breathing difficulty.* Watch out if a person's skin turns bluish or purplish

or if his breathing has stopped, is weak and shallow, or is raspy, rattling, or noisy.

Fever. Any temperature above 100°F (38°C) indicates danger when drugs or alcohol are involved.

Abnormal or irregular pulse. A pulse that is irregular or that falls above or below 60 to 120 beats per minute in an adult indicates danger.

Vomiting while not fully conscious. A person who is stuporous or unconscious runs a high risk of breathing vomited material into his lungs, creating serious breathing difficulties.

Convulsions. You can tell if a person is about to have a convulsion: he experiences muscle rigidity; muscle spasms; or twitching of the face, trunk, arms, or legs. A person who is experiencing a series of violent jerking movements or spasms is having a convulsion.

FIRST AID MEASURES

While you wait for medical help to arrive you can perform some first aid measures to alleviate the six danger signs listed above.

UNCONSCIOUSNESS   An unconscious person who is having convulsions or who is not breathing should have those emergencies handled first. If the person is breathing normally, try the following.

1. Loosen any tight clothing at the person's neck and waist.
2. If the person's jaw is relaxed remove his dentures or dental plates if he has them.
3. *Never* try to make the person drink anything.
4. *Never* try to make an unconscious person vomit.
5. Try to awaken the person by gently slapping or shaking him. *Do not* try to awaken a person who is twitching or having muscle spasms; you could bring on a seizure.
6. Turn the person on his side with his face pointing downward so that vomited material or mucus can drain freely from his mouth.

BREATHING DIFFICULTIES   Begin mouth-to-mouth ventilation immediately. Don't stop until the person is breathing on his own or until medical help has arrived and taken over the ventilation.

FEVER   Do what you can to lower the person's temperature: moisten the person's entire body with cool, wet cloths or with rubbing alcohol. Alcohol evaporates quickly and cools the body more rapidly. If you don't have rubbing alcohol use anything with alcohol in it, including whiskey.

IRREGULAR PULSE   If the pulse rate is high keep the person cool; if he is conscious, give him something cool to drink that does not contain caffeine. If the pulse is slow keep the person quiet.

CONVULSIONS   Keep the person from hurting himself. Place him on the floor, loosen any tight clothing, and remove dentures or dental plates if his jaw is relaxed. Place the person on his side; grasp his tongue and pull it forward (use a piece of cloth so you can maintain your grip) and place a wedge between the person's teeth if you can.

Never leave a victim of drug or alcohol abuse unattended; send others to obtain supplies or help. As you deal with the person remain calm and non-judmental, stressing your desire to help him return to normalcy so that he can be comfortable.

Drug and alcohol abuse have become major public health problems in the United States. Abuse not only presents medical problems but also presents serious psychological, emotional, and social problems. The effects of drug abuse can be worsened by factors such as method of taking the drug, concurrent illness, withdrawal, treatment onset, other life traumas, and stress.

As a helper, you may be called upon to deal with a drug or alcohol abuser. It is important to provide first aid as well as to give support. It is especially critical to be calm, reassuring, concerned, confident, caring, and encouraging. This can aid an abuser in his ultimate recovery from the damaging effects of alcohol and drugs.

13

DISASTERS

Disasters vary in kind, in length of the warning period, in number of people affected, in duration of impact, in extent of property damage, in number of casualties, and in many other ways. You may be involved with a flood that results suddenly when a dam bursts on a reservoir, giving only minutes' warning and wiping out an entire town. Or you may be involved in helping residents of a small rural town rebuild their homes after a tornado sweeps through with a day or two of advance warning.

Because each disaster is different, and because all the circumstances surrounding each disaster are different, it will take the victims different amounts of time to recover. You will need to be sensitive to their unique problems. Chances are, you will have been affected by the disaster, too, which places you in a good position: you can empathize. You're one of them, and the roof was ripped off the top of *your* house, too.

So much depends on the kind of disaster that strikes. Disasters such as earthquakes, tornadoes, hurricanes, and other storms are usually short and sharp and have little or no warning. Disasters such as natural floods, volcanoes, and tidal waves, on the other hand, are more likely to have impacts of longer duration and with at least some warning period. If the disaster strikes a large urban community there may be a number of services and trained personnel available for mounting a response; if the disaster strikes a rural area there may be few or no services available. These variations affect the kinds of emergency problems that appear.

It is normal to react to a disaster by doing something about it; victims usually "collect" themselves and then go about doing something to resolve the situation. With few exceptions, victims experience fear; many feel shaky, perspire profusely, become confused, and feel slightly nauseated. Those reactions are normal. As soon as the victims begin working to remedy the disaster situation their physical responses become less exaggerated and they are more able to work with less tension and fear.

But some reactions to disaster are abnormal.

1. *Physical reactions.* Physical reactions involve actual changes in body function, such as shakiness, fast pulse, abnormal breathing, nausea, and vomiting. While it is normal to experience some of these briefly the reaction becomes severe when the symptoms become prolonged or deep set, when they appear before the disaster actually occurs, or when they cannot be remedied. These kinds of physical reactions prevent a victim from acting responsibly in his own behalf or in helping others.

2. *Panic reactions.* Victims who become panicked act abnormally; they lose control, run around aimlessly with total disregard for safety (both theirs and others'), become reckless in their behavior, or weep so profusely that they become exhausted and unable to care for themselves, even if their lives depend on it.

3. *Overactive reactions.* While some amount of running around and confusion is normal following a disaster, some victims overreact. Far from being a small part of the confusion, they actually add to it; they do things that are unnecessary or even harmful. They tell stupid jokes, talk excessively, become demanding and critical, or become overly confident. They are unable to carry out an assignment; they jump from job to job, brush aside any directions given them by rescue workers, and generally make a spectacle of themselves.

4. *Depressed reactions.* It is normal to feel dazed, shocked, or numbed after a disaster occurs, but it is also normal to overcome those feelings quite quickly. Some victims are unable to "shake" these feelings; they act as if they are all alone in the world, and they move slowly and aimlessly. They generally do not respond to physical or verbal stimuli, and usually show no emotion—only a blank stare. These people are completely helpless and unaware of their surroundings, and they may wander into a dangerous situation that could further the disaster.

Usually the people who are reacting normally are those who are able to follow directions, who can respond in a helpful way, and who—if left on their own—will seek to do something truly helpful.

PHASES OF DISASTER

Historically, emphasis has been on the division of disasters into the phases of warning, threat, impact, inventory, rescue, remedy, and recovery. Let's examine each in detail.

Warning

Some disasters will be preceded by a minimal warning; these include cases of sudden onset, such as earthquake, flash flooding, or major explosion. But in other cases the gradual onset of the disaster—such as a flood that is preceded by a slowly swelling river and weeks of unusually heavy rainfall—allows for more time between the warning and the actual onset of the disaster. Of course, this warning contributes to heightened anxiety and apprehension.

Some people react to a warning as if the disaster had already occurred. Many of these have already been through a similar disaster at some other time in their lives; others are the kind of people who *always* become helpless in dangerous or frightening situations. Some people are able to act more effectively when they are under stress.

The people who become helpless should be first on the priority list of treatment, and aid should be offered so that they do not become hysterical or paralyzed by fear of their own helplessness. They may become a major source of problems if they are not attended to.You should assign them definite tasks; give them very clear and simple instructions, and reassure them that they are valuable and helpful in the situation. Let them know that they are important to everyone's safety and that they are *not* helpless. By giving them a job to do you will be able to remove any thoughts of helplessness they may have.

Threat

During the period of threat the danger becomes imminent. Behavioral reactions may be based on a number of considerations, such as an appraisal of whether the threat is real, how quickly the threat will materialize, how the disaster will affect the individual, what courses of action are available to ensure safety, what the costs of escape will be emotionally as well as physically and financially, and how everyone else is acting. Behavior at this point is apt to be very complex and is usually motivated by a network of causes.

Impact

When the disaster actually strikes any questions or doubts will be resolved. People will know *exactly* what the extent is and how they are being affected. The impact will be followed by some confusion while people adjust to what has happened.

Most victims will not panic, but they will experience fear and will rely on recognized leaders to provide them with instructions and guidance. You can be a leader that people will respond to, and it may be your responsibility to organize the victims so that they are included in the rescue work.

When victims are left without leadership several of them will generally appoint themselves as leaders and will go about the task of organizing the group. Although these individuals have not previously served as leaders in the community or among the group, the individuals in the group will generally respond to them as they would to recognized, established leaders.

Reactions of individuals at this point will range all the way from tension and disorganization to disorientation, confusion, feelings of hopelessness, or agitation and anger.

Inventory

In the inventory stage, more than at any other time during the disaster process, effective action can prevent further injury and save lives. You can act immediately to prevent disability, reduce abnormal behavior, and generally reduce the confusion. On the other hand, ineffective behavior at this time can exact terrible penalties. During the period of inventory victims and rescue workers determine exactly what has really happened. The disaster itself will be assessed.

Initial responses will probably include multiple physical complaints, fantasy and delusions, withdrawal from reality, nightmares, depression, apathy, chronic anxiety or fear, anger, or feelings of social fragmentation. Most will experience one or more of these reactions briefly but will return quickly to a normal level of reaction. Others will become stabilized at a level of moderate or serious disability. If the stress from the disaster is severe enough some may experience symptoms for the rest of their lives. Symptoms may even be passed on to offspring.

At first victims are split into small groups. But as rescue efforts are organized most victims will unite into a group that presents a strong front toward remedying the situation. Often what is mistaken for mass confusion is simply many individuals who are not united in a single activity but who are engaged in helpful and meaningful activities on their own.

Rescue

As a beginning to rescue work it is important to impress upon the victims that the menace has passed, that they are safe now. Those who cannot speak or who are otherwise seriously injured should be especially promptly attended to. By simply knowing that the disaster has passed they will feel more secure and will be able to regain a sense of well-being.

Behavior of the victims at this point will be dependent upon the severity of the disaster, the extent of victim involvement, facilities available for care, and other factors related to rescue, such as transportation and supplies available.

The focus and intent of the period of rescue is on helping the survivors cope with the disaster's aftermath. Some will lapse into shock, but most will be capable of handling the emergency and of helping reverse its effects. Only a few will suffer serious emotional problems; these will be manifest in the form of apathy, withdrawal, and regressed ability to think and act on their own.

Remedy

The remedy period of a disaster is the longest; during this period survivors and relief agencies conduct the activities designed to repair the stricken community. In some disasters the physical damage is slight but in most it is severe and requires a long time to repair. During this period the victim experience heightened morale, a cooperative spirit of helpfulness, and the desire to pitch in and be of assistance in the general cleanup and repair. During this period, too, those with severe physical or emotional injuries undergo the long process of rehabilitation. Some experience emotional crises that they did not experience earlier. Some people are composed and strong under stress, but lose control afterward; deep emotional problems may surface six months to a year after the disaster.

WHO IS INVOLVED?

Remember, the people involved in a disaster are "normal" people. True, some people will react adversely to the disaster, and will display behavior that varies widely from what we usually consider normal, but most of the people involved are just like you—they are your neighbors, your friends, your family members. You won't have to work with those who are extremely disturbed, except to help them get professional help quickly; most of your work will be with normal people who are suffering normal stress. Keeping this in mind will make your task more realistic and approachable.

Some of the most important help you render will be simply listening, indicating interest and concern for someone else's problems. Remember these principles.

1. People generally do not disintegrate in a disaster. There is usually a short stage of panic, but once that clears you will find people pitching in, helping others, and working hard. Remember, too, that this won't last forever. If the recovery from the disaster takes weeks or months, those involved will become disillusioned and discouraged after a while. Many of those around you will be stronger than you think and able to pitch in and help.

2. People respond to active interest and concern. One of the greatest fears of a person who is undergoing great stress is that he will be abandoned or isolated; many feel that they are alone in their problems, even though they are obviously surrounded by hundreds of others who are in the same predicament. Take time to sit down and listen to any person's problems; it may seem almost humorous at the time but this person is genuinely convinced that he's the only one who has it bad at the time. Try to find a quiet place where you can talk, away from the confusion. Establish good eye contact with the person, and sit in a comfortable posture, leaning slightly forward. As he talks to you periodically repeat something in your own words to demonstrate that you understand and to give him the opportunity to clarify or add information. Take care not to judge the person or be critical of what he is telling you—to him, these are valid, genuine feelings. He needs someone to understand and to accept him for them.

Remember that you may need to listen to an account of the disaster many times in the course of helping many people. Listen to each person as if it were the first time you had heard the story; listen patiently if the same person needs to tell the story several times.

3. People may reject help because of pride; you need to use tact and sensitivity. Some people interpret help as an admission of weakness; they'd rather struggle along than admit they need the help. Here's where you are lucky—you're a neighbor, someone who understands, someone who needs help, too. Try to involve the people as a team whenever you can instead of just extending help—"Come on, Frank. Can you get your three kids to help me clear this debris away from the porch?" Make the person feel valuable, and make him feel that he is helping you as much as you are asking for help.

4. Ambivalence is a human characteristic. A person who is under emotional stress can be expected to feel opposing or conflicting feelings at the same time; sometimes the feelings oscillate rapidly. Anticipate this; then help the person recognize that this is normal and acceptable, and that it will pass with time. Listen carefully to the person, and help him distinguish between his feelings; help him decide which feeling is most important, and which should be acted on first. Above all, strive to help him understand that he is not mentally ill or emotionally unstable because of these different feelings.

GENERAL GUIDELINES FOR DISASTER MANAGEMENT

While each disaster presents individual problems some guidelines are general and will apply to any disaster you may be called to respond to.

1. Don't let yourself become overwhelmed by the immensity of the disaster. Move slowly from one person to another; this will help you stay calm and will help you feel that you are making progress.

2. Obtain and distribute information about the disaster and the victims if you can. The families of victims deserve accurate information about both the disaster and the victims; encourage medical authorities on the scene to provide this quickly. You might work with several others to gather records and information so this process can be speeded up.

3. Reunite victims with their families as soon as you can. There are two benefits to this: first, emotional stress will be lessened once victims are with their family members. Second, family members may be able to provide you with information that will help you deal better with the victims. If the victims have been seriously injured you will need to handle the reunion with tact; prepare the family ahead of time for what they will see so that they do not react with shock—"Part of Alan's face was burned in the explosion; the medics have bandaged it, but you will be able to see some large blisters around his eye that are yellow and that have liquid draining from them. These are not painful for Alan at this time, and they will probably heal without leaving a scar."

4. Encourage victims who are able to do necessary chores. Work can be therapeutic and should be used to help victims get over their own problems. You might think that victims are unable to do any work because their condition appears to render them unfit; but many victims simply do not know what to do first and are generally overwhelmed by the disaster.

Help victims devise a schedule to perform their own daily routines like they did before the disaster. Impress upon them the importance of resuming an aura of normality as soon as possible. In addition, give them simple, clear instructions and let them help you perform some rescue tasks. Recognize the fact that their responses may be slightly depressed; be patient with them and give only one instruction at a time.

5. If the disaster has involved a large number of people, group the victims with their families and neighbors. This will help reduce feelings of fear and alienation.

6. Provide a structure for the emotionally injured and let them know what your expectations are. Let the victims know exactly what is happening to them; tell them that they are suffering a temporary setback, that they are likely to recover rapidly, and that meanwhile you expect them to perform certain minimal tasks. Explain those tasks clearly and simply, and then follow up to make sure they are performing them.

7. Help the victims confront the reality of the disaster. You have two responsibilities here: one is to help the victims face reality, and the other is to help the victims take their minds off the crisis. Many times victims assume the worst. Help the victims work through their feelings. Encourage them to talk about the disaster and what they feel will be the long-term effects. If you sense that the victims are not facing reality or that their expectations are much worse than reality, help them adjust their views.

8. Discourage people from using sedatives and drugs. Many victims will need a tranquilizer to help them over the initial shock of the disaster, but it is dangerous to keep taking tranquilizers, because the victims won't be able to heal emotionally as long as they are sedated. People need to go through the process of resolution and remedy, and they can't while they're on drugs.

9. Don't give false assurances. The victims don't need a false promise that things will work out all right—instead, they need help in facing the problems and help in deciding how they will react to their problems. They need to face facts sooner or later; if they find out that you have lied to them they may totally resist further help, and their recovery period will probably be extensive. Honestly appraise the situation for the victims and then offer to help in areas where they feel they need it. Express your confidence in the victims' ability to overcome the situation and handle the crisis.

10. Permit the victims limited dependency. Explain that accepting help is not a sign of weakness. Make sure they understand that the help (and, therefore, their dependence) is only temporary and that as soon as things are under control *they* may be needed to help someone else.

11. Arrange for a group discussion where victims can exchange ideas as soon as the physical needs are taken care of.

12. Identify people who are in a unique position to help those in need and recruit them and train them in psychological first aid.

13. Make sure that you use existing community resources; physicians, teachers, business leaders, clergy, union leaders, public service personnel, and community volunteers can all be mobilized to help victims of a disaster.

14. Help minimize the psychological stress on the rescue workers. Establish set schedules for each rescue worker, and make sure that each one takes rest breaks regularly, even if they are brief. Organize the crew so that there is a supervisor, someone who is not working directly with the victims and whose job it is to recognize symptoms of stress in the rescue workers. If a rescue worker does start developing signs of undue stress instruct the supervisor to remove the rescue worker from the situation, impose a longer-than-normal rest period, and return the rescue worker to a less stressful situation. During the rest periods make food and drink available to the rescue workers; encourage them to talk to each other about their experiences and feelings. If time is available make sure they get some sleep.

Rescue workers should not be given medication or drugs of any kind unless they first check with the supervisor. If they are unable to handle the situation without medication remove them to a less stressful assignment.

GROUPS WITH SPECIAL NEEDS

Because of their age, their economic background, or their cultural or racial background, some victims of disaster will need special help.

Children

Young children may exhibit a number of unusual reactions to a disaster; most commonly, they will regress to a period of young childhood. You will be able to tell when this is happening: a nine-year-old will start wetting the bed, for example. The children may have some physical reactions: loss of appetite, bowel or bladder problems, sleep disorders, headaches, muscle spasms, stammering or stuttering, or problems with eyesight or hearing. They will probably have some emotional reactions, too: withdrawal from friends and the normal play group, fear of school, refusal to leave their parents, loss of interest in activities that used to fascinate them, inability to concentrate, or fighting with siblings or close friends.

Children need plenty of physical comforting after a disaster strikes; be prepared to hold and caress a child if he acts like he wants it. Even if he doesn't want you to hold him soothe him verbally by telling him how much you like him.

Make sure the child's physical comforts are taken care of. Give him some warm milk to help comfort him. If he is frightened let him sleep in his parents' room for a few nights.

Encourage the child to express his feelings about the disaster. You may need to role play; have a group of children act out the disaster, assigning each a role.

Encourage the child to perform chores that he would normally do. If it is his responsibility to milk the cow, for instance, encourage him to do that now. If he normally clears the dishes from the table help him do that and talk to him about his feelings while you work together.

Adolescents

Teenagers will suffer fewer physical symptoms than children; some common ones include skin rash, digestive disorders, and reappearance of earlier speech habits. The emotional reactions of adolescents are often severe; they compete with younger brothers and sisters for the attention of parents, fail to carry out chores, lose interest in sexual activity, lose interest in social activities with friends, lose interest in hobbies and recreation, sharply resist parental or school authority, suffer a marked decline in physical activity, encounter difficulty in concentrating, and express feelings of inadequacy and helplessness.

It's important to give special, additional attention and consideration to adolescents. Too often they are passed over in disaster because they appear to be adult enough to handle their problems. Take extra measure to make the adolescent feel secure.

Give the adolescent increased responsibility as long as he can comfortably handle it. You might ask him to help rehearse others on safety or evacuation procedures; provide structured but undemanding activities for him that will give him a sense of purpose.

Encourage the teenager to associate with others his own age and to resume some group activity; temporarily lower your expectations of him as far as schoolwork and other performance are concerned. It is critical at this time that he build his self-esteem and that he avoid failure experiences.

It is sometimes hard for an adolescent to express his feelings; work with him to help him communicate his feelings about the disaster. You might get a group of adolescents together and initiate a kind of group discussion or forum that will help all of them vent their frustrations and confront their feelings.

Middle-aged Adults

Middle-aged adults react to disaster with a host of emotions: withdrawal, anger, irritability, and apathy. Sometimes one person can experience conflicting emotions at the same time.

This age group's greatest problem is with psychosomatic illness, physical or imagined physical illness caused by emotional stress. Most commonly seen in disasters are ulcers, diabetes, and heart problems that result directly from emotional stress and inability to handle the crisis situation. Other physical symptoms suffered by the middle-aged adults during a disaster include loss of interest in everyday activities; loss of apetite; and sleep problems, problems falling asleep and problems staying asleep.

You will need to acknowledge and confront physical symptoms and signs of distress; encourage the person to seek medical help, and arrange for a doctor if the person does not already have one. If you ignore the physical ailments, even if you believe they are imaginary, you are telling the victim that his problems are not real and that they are not worthy of your time and consideration.

Once the person's medical problems are attended to encourage him to talk to someone he trusts about the feelings he has; this could be a close family friend, a family physician, a minister, or another family member. If you think the person needs professional help encourage him to accept it and then help him locate it. You may need to help him arrange for financial assistance if he chooses to seek professional help.

Keep the other family members informed as to what is happening with the person; encourage them to communicate freely with the victim, and help them be open and honest with their feelings. Alert the family to possible danger signals, especially to the physical signs of extensive depression, and let them know that you are available for help whenever they need it.

The Elderly

The elderly, too, suffer with physical complaints during a disaster; the number of their physical complaints will probably increase, and their physical condition may decline sharply.

One of the most difficult aspects of the elderly person's reaction is confusion, disorientation, and memory loss; the person may react with hostility, anger, agitation, apathy, or suspicion from confusion and the inability to remember. Depression is a big problem with the elderly.

It is critical that you help re-establish normalcy for the elderly as quickly as possible. If the home was destroyed rescue as many familiar possessions as you can, and return them to the person; arrange for suitable relocation as quickly as you can, and put familiar objects in the new home.

The elderly will be much more dependent than others will be. You will probably need to arrange for transportation, and you may need to escort the person everywhere for the first few weeks. Give special attention to helping the person establish his social contacts again; reuniting him with friends and family members can provide stability amidst the confusion.

Provide strong verbal reassurance to the elderly person. Tell him, over and over again, what is happening; express your belief that he will be strong enough to pull through the crisis. Make sure he understands that you are there to help and that you will not desert him.

Lower-Income Groups

Members of lower-income groups tend to seek medical help only in time of crisis or disaster; unless you are aggressive and go to them they likely will not seek emotional support of any kind. Stress that you are a friend or neighbor and that you are lending support because you care for them and want to work with them so that all of you can survive the disaster well. Emphasize that there is no charge for your help; perhaps you can make them feel that they are helping you.

Upper-Income Groups

You may encounter some resistance from members of upper-income groups; they may be reluctant to accept "free" help in a disaster. They may want to pay you for your help, or they may insist on seeing a professional for help. If there are professionals available encourage them to seek the professionals and help them locate a professional if they desire that kind of help. If there are no professionals available stress that all of you need to work together to support each other; you will not pay them, and they needn't pay you.

Cultural or Racial Minorities

If you can arrange for a member of their own subgroup to help members of a cultural or racial minority; there will be less suspicion, less frustration over language and cultural barriers, and less failure in efforts to help. If no such person is available treat the situation with delicacy and tact; you will need increased understanding and patience as you work through the problems the crisis has created.

Institutionalized Persons

Because they can't move around freely institutionalized persons usually react to a disaster with frustration, fear, and panic; they are helplessly dependent on those who are caring for them in the institution.

To help alleviate anxiety, help the person contact a friend or a member of his family; he will know that they are safe, and they will know he is safe. Provide him with as much information about the disaster as you can, and reassure him that things will eventually be better.

If the institution has been endangered or demolished by the disaster help the people find suitable housing, and help them contact their families with information on where they are. Encourage them to help clean up or to participate in other simple tasks.

Provide opportunities for the people in the institution to get together in a group and to discuss their feelings about the disaster. People in this situation can really benefit from group discussion; they realize clearly that they are not alone in their frustrations, fears, and panic, and they understand that these feelings are normal. Help them understand that their feelings are temporary and that they will pass with time.

FOUR PRINCIPLES TO REMEMBER

Four basic principles will help you in dealing with a disaster situation.

1. *Respect everyone's right to have his own feelings.* You probably will not feel like many of the victims you treat; you may have different value systems and different morals, and you may be convinced that you would certainly act differently if you were in this situation. *Remember, though, that the victim's feelings are real to him.* Don't judge, censor, or ridicule. Instead, try to understand how the victim is feeling so that you will know best how to help him. People are the products of a wide variety of factors—you can't possibly know what influence has made an individual what he is. So quit trying to figure him out. Instead, try to relate to how he feels, and try to figure out how you can help him. Remember, people do not *like* being confused and upset; they would snap out of it if they could. Your role is to help as much as possible without rejecting and ridiculing.

2. *Accept the fact that emotional disability is as real as physical disability.* If a man's leg is ripped off in an automobile accident no one, including the man himself, expects him to get up and walk away. But that mistake is too often made with victims of emotional disability. Those victims are expected to recover spontaneously and without any residual effects. Rescue workers snap orders: "It's all in your head!" "Come on, get control of yourself!" "Buck up!" Provide support for the victim, but at the same time acknowledge that his disability, his emotional sickness, is very real and very difficult for him to handle. Try to be patient and help the victim work through his problems at his own pace. He will resolve them as quickly as he can—again, no one *likes* being upset and confused.

3. *Realize that every physically handicapped person is also emotionally injured.* Any victim of a physical injury will also have a strong emotional reaction to that injury. Even a slight injury, such as a cut finger, gives a person a slight start. Realize that the injured person will be upset; and the more severe his injury, the more upset he will be. Some people will be more upset about injuries to certain parts of the body; a baseball pitcher, for instance, will be much more upset about a relatively minor injury to his hand than would a marathon runner with the same hand injury. Most people will become severely upset over any injury to the eyes or genitals.

4. *Realize that most victims are stronger than they look.* Victims of a disaster are crippled by a temporary feeling of shock, confusion, anguish, pain, and fear. They probably will not put their best foot forward at first. It is up to you to help them in any way they need to regain their emotional stability. Once you have helped a person he will likely become strong, helpful, cooperative and intelligent again.

INDEX

A

Abnormal grief, 41
Abortion, 62, 70-79
  counseling and, 75-78
  physical and emotional adjustment to,
    72-75
  reasons for, 70-72
  refusing, 78-79
  suicide and, 78
Abram, Harry S., 135n
Acceptance, 21-22
Accidents, 6
Active crisis, state of, 4-5
Adolescents:
  depression and, 111-12
  disaster and, 157
  suicide and, 112, 118-20, 122-29
Alcoholism, 82, 108, 141-47
  first aid measures, 146-47

  hostility, handling, 145
  medical danger signs, 145-46
  reactions to, 142-43
American Medical Association, 60
American Psychiatric Association, 117
American Psychological Association, 117
Anger, 20, 37, 44-45, 93
Anniversary crisis, 7
Anticipatory grief, 40-41
Antidepressant drugs, 111, 130
Aquilera, Donna, C., 6n
Awareness stage of grief, 36-38

B

Backer, Dorothy, 92n
Bard, Bernard, 57n
Bard, Morton, 5n
Bargaining, 20-21
Behavioral signs of crisis, 16

Berg, Donald E., 124n
Borgman, Robert, 85n
Brain death, 61
Breathing difficulties, 145-46
Burgess, Anne Wolbert, 88n, 89n, 92n
Burgoyne, R. W., 109n

C

Cassem, Ned H., 22n
Cellular death, 61
Charmaz, Kathy, 19n
Child abuse, 80-87
  counseling and, 83-87
  factors leading to, 81-82
  identification of, 83
Children:
  depression in 110-11
  disaster and, 156-57
  dying, 29-34
  explaining death to, 28-29
  grief and mourning and, 42-49
  working with, 13-14
  (*see also* Adolescents; Child abuse)
Clinical death, 61
Cohen, David, 113n
Cohen, John, 116n
Convulsions, 146, 147
Coping mechanisms, 9
Crib death, 52-54
Crime, 5
Crisis:
  definition of, 1-2
  effecting change in, 9-13
  elements of, 3-5
  predictable, 5
  signs and symptoms of, 13-14
  support system, 6-9
  unpredictable, 5-6
Crisis intervention, definition of, 2
Curphey, Theodore, 119n

D

Davis, Carolyn, 77n
Davoren, Elizabeth, 83n, 84n
Death and dying, 2, 6, 18-34
  dying children, 29-34
  explaining death to children, 28-29
  meeting needs, 25-28
  needs of dying person, 22-24
  rights of dying person, 24-25
  stages of, 19-22, 61
  (*see also* Euthanasia: Grief and mourning)
Denes, Magda, 78n
Denial, 20, 36
Depressed reactions to disaster, 149-50

Depression, 21, 40, 91, 107-17
  in adolescents, 111-12
  in children, 110-11
  counseling for, 116-17
  definition of, 107
  incidence of, 108
  postnatal, 112-15
  prevention of, 117
  signs and symptoms of, 108-9
Diran, Margaret O'Keefe, 120n
Disasters, 5-6, 148-61
  adolescents and, 157
  children and, 156-57
  elderly and, 158
  guidelines for management, 154-56, 160-61
  middle-aged adults and, 157-58
  phases of, 150-52
  reactions to, 149-50
  socioeconomic status and, 159
Divorce, 6, 54-55
Drug abuse, 82, 108, 141-47
  first aid measures, 146-47
  hostility, handling, 145
  medical danger signs, 145-46
  reactions to, 142-43
Dying children, 29-34

E

Earley, Kathleen, 116n
Economic resources, 9
Edmunds, Margaret, 85n
Elderly persons:
  disaster and, 158
  suicide and, 119-21, 129-31
Electroshock therapy, 130
Elliott, Neil, 60n, 64n
Emergencies, psychiatric, 97-106
  principles of management, 100-106
Emotional aspects of illness, 134-40
Emotional resources, 3
Emotional signs of crisis, 15
Emotional stages of dying, 19-22
Environment, control of, 11
Euthanasia, 56-69
  arguments against, 67-69
  arguments for, 64-67
  kinds of, 63-64, 67
Events, perception of, 7-8

F

Failure to thrive syndrome, 110
Falk, Marshall A., 110n
Family, as support system, 8-9
Family life experience, 6

Farberow, Norman L., 119*n*
Fever, 146
First aid measures, 146-47
Fletcher, Joseph, 57*n*
Frederick, Calvin J., 100*n*, 126*n*
Friedman, Cornelia Morrison, 76*n*
Funerals, 47, 52
Furman, Erna, 42*n*

G

Gaffney, Kathleen F., 49*n*
Garrard, Robert L., 130
Gilson, George S., 49*n*
Glover, Benjamin H., 97*n*
"Go-along" technique, 99
Godenne, Ghislaine D., 112*n*
Green, Helen I., 143*n*
Greenblatt, Milton, 40*n*
Grief and mourning, 35-55
 abnormal, 41
 anticipatory, 40-41
 children and, 42-49
 coping with, 41-42
 infants, death of, 50-54
 normal reactions, 36-40
 parents and, 49-50
 spouse, loss of, 54-55
 (*see also* Death and dying)
Guilt, 37, 44, 45, 51, 53, 93, 95
Gunther, Jane, 54*n*

H

Habgood, J. S., 67*n*, 68*n*
Hafen, Brent Q., 7*n*, 8*n*, 10*n*, 36*n*, 37*n*,
 100*n*
Hatton, Corrine Loing, 133*n*
Hay, Pamela, 36*n*, 37*n*
Hayman, Charles R., 92*n*
Hazardous event, 4
Hefter, Gilbert M., 100*n*
Held, Mark L., 29*n*
Helmrath, Thomas, 49*n*
Hilgers, Thomas W., 72*n*
Holmstrom, Lynda Lytle, 88*n*, 92*n*
Homosexuality, 108
Hope, 3, 12

I

Idealization stage of grief, 39-40
Illness, emotional aspects of, 134-40
Immediate help, 10-11
Impact of disaster, 151

Infants:
 death of, 50-54
 depression and, 110
Institutionalized persons, disaster and,
 159-60
Intellectual functions, 3
Interest, loss of, 109
International Childbirth Association, 114
Interpersonal assets, 3
Inventory of disaster, 151-52

J

Jackson, Edgar N., 42*n*
Johnston, Daniel, 2*n*

K

Kalmar, Roberta, 76*n*
Karren, Keith J., 100*n*
Kennell, John H., 50*n*
Keyserlingk, Edward W., 66*n*, 67*n*, 68*n*
Klagsbrun, Francine, 121*n*
Kubler-Ross, Elizabeth, 19*n*

L

La Leche League, 114
Lanza, Charlene, 92*n*
Lascari, Andre D., 29*n*
Lauer, James W., 85*n*
Learned aggression, 81
Levy, Jerome S., 135*n*
Levy, Michael H., 143*n*
Listening, 12-13
Litman, Robert E., 119*n*
Littlewood, Barbara, 36*n*
Lothane, Zvi, 135*n*
Lowery, Patti, 143*n*
Luparello, Thomas J., 135*n*

M

MacDicken, Robert A., 85*n*
Maher-Loughnan, G. P., 135*n*
Matthews, Robert A., 100*n*
McGrory, Arlene, 25*n*
Medical danger signs, 145-46
Mental Health Association, 117
Messick, Janice M., 6*n*
Middle-aged adults, disaster and, 157-58
Miles, Margaret S., 49*n*
Miller, Mary Susan, 118*n*, 120*n*
Mood changes, 108
Morris, Terry, 68*n*
Mourning (*see* Grief and mourning)

N

Nafulin, Donald H., 108*n*
Natural disasters (*see* Disasters)
National Institute of Mental Health, 117
Needs of dying persons, 22-28
Newton, Michael, 114*n*
Normal grief reactions, 36-40
Notification, 6

O

Olsen, Patricia, 100*n*
Overactive reactions to disaster, 149

P

Panic reactions to disaster, 149
Parad, Howard J., 8*n*
Parents, grief and mourning and, 49-50
Parry-Jones, W. L., 108*n*
Paulson, George W., 63*n*
Personality, healthy, 3
Physical reactions to disasters, 149
Physical signs of crisis, 14-15
Postnatal depression, 112-15
Precipitating factor, 4
Predictable crises, 5
Pregnancy, 72, 78
    physical and emotional adjustment to, 72
    suicide and, 78
Pretzel, Paul W., 121*n*
Psychiatric emergencies, 97-106
    principles of management, 100-106
Psychotic reactions, 6
Pulse rate, 146-147
Puryear, Douglas A., 10*n*

Q

Quinlan, Karen Anne, 65

R

Rabiner, Charles J., 135*n*
Rachlis, David, 129*n*
Rape and sexual assault, 88-96
    counseling and, 92-96
    reactions to, 89-92
Remedy period of disaster, 152
Rescue work, 152, 156
Resnik, H. L. P., 123*n*, 143*n*
Resolution stage of grief, 38-39
Restitition stage of grief, 38
Rhodes, Ronald L., 7*n*, 8*n*, 10*n*
Rights of dying persons, 24-25

Rosslyn, Virginia, 108*n*, 116*n*
Rowland, Lloyd W., 100*n*
Ruben, Diane Daskal, 143*n*

S

Schneidman, Edwin S., 35*n*, 119*n*
Schulz, John, 143*n*
Schulz, Richard, 40*n*
See, Carolyn, 88*n*
Segal, Julius, 110*n*
Self-concept, negative, 108
Self-esteem, 7, 111-12
Self-image, 12
Self-motivation, 3
Self-reliance, 12
Separation, 6
Sexual assault (*see* Rape and Sexual assault)
Sheer, Barbara Lee, 29*n*
Shub, Mark G., 100*n*
Shultz, John B., 2*n*
Sloane, R. Bruce, 78*n*, 109*n*
Smilkstein, Gabriel, 6*n*, 9*n*
Smith, Dorothy W., 135*n*
Smith, Mary L., 116*n*
Social network, 8-9
Socioeconomic status, disaster and, 159
Soreff, Stephen, 100*n*
Spouse, loss of, 54-55
Steinmetz, S. K., 81*n*
Stewart, Rege S., 22*n*
Stratton, John, 92*n*
Stress, 2-5, 81-82, 143
Striffler, Russell C., 135*n*
Sudden Infant Death Syndrome (SIDS),
    52-54
Suicide, 6, 108, 118-33
    adolescents and, 112, 118-20, 122-29
    elderly and, 119-21, 129-31
    postnatal depression and, 113
    pregnant women and, 78
    prevention, 131-33
Support systems, 6-9, 12, 74

T

Tabachnick, Norman, 119*n*
Thompson, Lois, 36*n*, 37*n*
Threat of disaster, 150-51
Thygerson, Alton L., 7*n*, 8*n*, 10*n*

U

Unconsciousness, 145, 146
Unpredictable crises, 5-6

V

Vomiting, 146
Vulnerable state, 4

W

Warning of disaster, 150
Watt, Anne S., 42n, 43n
Weinstein, Stanley E., 52n

Wessel, Morris A., 45n
Widowhood, 54-55
Willner, Allen E., 135n
Winickoff, Susan A., 123n

Z

Zucker, Karen Waugh, 61n
Zusman, Jac, 100n